A SHORT INTRODUCTION TO
PSYCHOTHERAPY

Short Introductions to the Therapy Professions
Series Editor: Colin Feltham

Books in this series examine the different professions which provide help for people experiencing emotional or psychological problems. Written by leading practitioners and trainers in each field, the books are a source of up-to-date information about

- the nature of the work
- training, continuing professional development and career pathways
- the structure and development of the profession
- client populations and consumer views
- research and debates surrounding the profession.

Short Introductions to the Therapy Professions are ideal for anyone thinking about a career in one of the therapy professions or in the early stages of training. The books will also be of interest to mental health professionals needing to understand allied professions and also to patients, clients and relatives of service users.

Books in the series:

A Short Introduction to Clinical Psychology
Katherine Cheshire and David Pilgrim

A Short Introduction to Psychoanalysis
Jane Milton, Caroline Polmear and Julia Fabricius

A Short Introduction to Psychiatry
Linda Gask

CONTENTS

INFORMATION ON THE EDITOR AND CONTRIBUTORS

Melanie Epstein MBBCh MRCPCH Dip Psych has worked as a psychotherapist in primary care and in private practice for 10 years. She has a longstanding interest in research developed during 20 years of medical practice working with children and families in a range of community and hospital settings. She has published and presented a range of paediatric-related research. She is the author of two chapters on child mental health in the paediatric Mastercourse series published by Elsevier. She was the research course leader at Northern Guild for Psychotherapy for 5 years. She has a private practice in Leeds.

Sarah Hamlyn has been working in the field of counselling and psychotherapy for 15 years. She is a trainer and supervisor of psychotherapists and for the past six years has been Programme Co-ordinator for Integrative Psychotherapy training at the Northern Guild for Psychotherapy. She has practised in a variety of settings including the University of Leeds, and NHS primary care. She has a private psychotherapy practice based in Leeds.

Robin Hobbes BA CQSW CTA TSTA is co-director of Elan Psychotherapy Training Institute. Located in Manchester, the Institute specialises in Transactional Analysis and Integrative Psychotherapy. He is currently the Chair of Clinical Practice and the former chairperson of the British Institute of Transactional Analysis. He lives in south Manchester and can be contacted at robin@elantraining.org.

Yvonne Lawrence BA CQSW MSW CTA Dip Psych is a UKCP-registered psychotherapist who has worked as a full-time integrative psychotherapist and counsellor for 16 years. She works in both private practice and NHS settings in the north-east of England. She is an experienced supervisor and teacher of psychotherapy, having taught for 12 years on the Northern Guild for Psychotherapy training programme to Master level. Her particular interest is in-depth work focusing on early developmental issues.

Christine Lister-Ford is a Director of the Northern Guild for Psychotherapy where she leads the MSc in Integrative Psychotherapy.

Previously she sat on the Governing Board of the United Kingdom Council for Psychotherapy for 7 years. She has chaired International and European Training Standards groups over a 15 year period. Her previous publications include *Skills in Transactional Analysis Counselling & Psychotherapy* (SAGE, 2002). She is a member of the editorial boards of several psychotherapy journals.

Tricia Scott MSc, MAHPP, UKCP-Fellow has worked with individuals, groups, couples and families in private, voluntary and statutory settings for over 30 years. She specialised in NHS practice for 10 years and currently leads the MA programmes at Bath Centre for Psychotherapy and Counselling. Her book *Integrative Psychotherapy in Healthcare: A Humanistic Approach* (Palgrave Macmillan) was published in 2004.

INTRODUCTION

Psychotherapy – a new profession

This is a very exciting time for psychotherapy. The field is developing and expanding. It has been well over half a century since we have seen such a burgeoning of ideas.

In writing this short introduction we want to provide a map of the field and focus on some of the key areas of growth. For many psychotherapists, introductory books like this one were thin on the ground when we set out on our own journey to qualification. At that time one of the best ways to find out about psychotherapy was to try a weekend workshop or join a group. The human potential movement which started in earnest in the 1960s gave unrivalled access to gaining first-hand experiential knowledge. 'Taste it and see' was a prevailing culture. In many ways this is probably still the best way to decide what feels right.

We hope that this introduction, like any short guide, will give you an overview of some of the important areas and a chance to find out more about them. All the authors are seasoned psychotherapists with years of experience under their belts. As practitioners in the field they bring hands-on knowledge and a real understanding of the depth and breadth of psychotherapeutic practice.

Structure

Chapters cover key areas of knowledge and practice ranging from theory to future developments in the field.

Chapter 1 looks at the fascinating historical weavings of theory and practice, practitioner and client. It is a brief but scholarly overview of developments in the field from Freud to the present day.

Chapter 2 considers applications of psychotherapy looking at a selection of schools and modalities in greater depth and comparing and contrasting some of these.

Chapter 3 considers the evidence base and points to the need for a full understanding of what research means in the psychotherapeutic therapeutic sphere. It considers different approaches to psychotherapy research and what these yield.

Chapter 4 critiques the field and takes an honest look at the profession.

Chapter 5 looks at psychotherapy practice in the NHS and includes some brief case studies.

Chapter 6 gives a breakdown of what is involved in training as a psychotherapist and describes in detail the path to qualification.

Finally, Chapter 7 looks to future trends and developments in the field and emphasises the need for new approaches to practise to meet increasingly diverse social needs.

Acknowledgements

My thanks to Colin Feltham, the series editor, for giving me the opportunity to write this book and allowing me to develop the book in my own way.

To Alison Poyner of Sage who has been available, flexible and responsive as the book neared completion.

To my fellow authors for their commitment and enthusiasm and generous sharing of their knowledge.

Christine Lister-Ford
Saltburn-by-the-Sea
April 2006

1

AN HISTORICAL OVERVIEW OF PSYCHOTHERAPY

SARAH HAMLYN

Early views of mental illness

Since the earliest recording of human culture there has been evidence of human mental and emotional distress and also ways to explain and alleviate it. Responses have ranged from demonisation and execution to some form of 'treatment'. Hippocrates in the third century BC considered that mental distress must have a physical cause. However, the predominant view in most cultures has been to define mental disturbance in terms of spiritual distress and the task of healing it has been seen as belonging to the realm of priests and of shamans who used trance states to effect emotional healing, for example through 'soul retrieval' (Ingerman, 1991).

The predominant Christian view of mental distress has been to regard it as caused by evil spirits, or as possession by demons. From the thirteenth century, the inquisition of the Catholic church defined people with deviant behaviour as possessed or as witches, and persecuted them. In 1487 *Malleus Maleficarum* (*The Witch Hammer*) was published. It attributed abnormal behaviour to satanic influences and specified the diagnosis, behaviour, trial and punishment of witches and provided a basis for the torture of people with deviant behaviour. Loss of reason was seen as a key diagnostic feature, and many hundreds of thousands of mentally disturbed individuals (suffering from what we would now think of as psychosis, and even depression) were tortured and put to death. Most of those who suffered were female and the authors of *Malleus Maleficarum* considered that 'All witchcraft comes from carnal lust, which in women is insatiable' (Tallis, 1998: 5).

It is also likely that some early Christian visionaries and saints suffered from mental illness. For example Joan of Arc may well have suffered auditory hallucinations. Interestingly she was both burned as a witch and, later, sanctified by the church – perhaps an indicator of the ambivalent and confused view of mental disturbance. The last execution of a witch took place in Switzerland as late as 1782 and it was around this time that more humane views of mental illness were emerging.

The beginnings of care and treatment

In Europe, alongside the religious view, there has also been the approach of containing the mentally ill. In 1247 the priory of St Mary of Bethlehem was founded in London. It later became known as Bethlehem Hospital (or 'Bedlam') and from as early as 1377 it was used to house 'distracted persons'. Treatment there was nevertheless based on the idea of possession by demons, resulting in the punitive and neglectful treatment of inmates.

At the time of the renaissance there is evidence of debate as to whether mental disturbance was a spiritual or a physical and medical problem. A well-known example of this may be found in Shakespeare's *Macbeth* (published in 1599). The doctor observes Lady Macbeth's troubled sleep-walking and responds:

'This disease is beyond my practice ...
　　... Unnatural deeds
Do breed unnatural troubles; infected minds
To their deaf pillows will discharge their secrets.
More needs she the divine than the physician' (*Macbeth*, V. i.)

thus placing mental disturbance firmly in the hands of spiritual care. He also suggests that problematic or traumatic events can lead to mental distress. When the doctor reports to Macbeth he receives the challenge:

　　　　　Cure her of that.
Canst thou not minister to a mind diseas'd,
Pluck from the memory a rooted sorrow,
Raze out the written troubles of the brain,
And with some sweet oblivious antidote
Cleanse the stuff'd bosom of that perilous stuff
Which weighs upon the heart? (*Macbeth*, V. iii.)

However, the doctor washes his hands of the problem:

　　　　Therein the patient
Must minister to himself (*Macbeth*, V. iii.)

Although Macbeth is clearly articulating the idea that mental distress has a cause and potentially a cure, this was, at the time Shakespeare wrote, a novel idea and the doctor here evidently does not regard healing the mind as within the province of medicine and science.

The implication is that talking (confession) with a priest is what is needed, and that there is no magic pill to cure such distress. This debate is still current, and while we now have effective psychotropic medications, the role of human relationship and contact through talking is acknowledged by both medicine and religion as being highly important in resolving distress and maintaining well-being.

In 1586, just 13 years before *Macbeth* was written, the first medical book about mental illness, the *Treatise on Melancholy* by a physician called Timothie Bright, was published. It contained descriptions of what we would now call depression or mood disorder, and may well have been a source for Shakespeare, particularly for *Hamlet*. In 1632 came the publication of Burton's *Anatomy of Melancholy*, and this included both descriptions and treatments (diet, exercise), based on earlier medical views. Burton wrote in order to relieve his own melancholy and considered it possible to alleviate this distress.

Despite these acknowledgements of the role of treatment, the predominant approach to mental distress continued to be incarceration and physical restraint. Patients might be chained or manacled, and treatments included blood-letting, whipping and immersion in cold water. Furthermore, in the seventeenth century the behaviour of mentally deranged people was considered amusing and Bethlehem Hospital was open to the public who could take a tour and view the inmates as a form of entertainment. John Evelyn described a visit in his diary in 1657: 'several poor miserable creatures in chains; one of them was mad with making verses'. Hogarth's 1735 picture of Bedlam shows the kind of scene these tourists might have observed. Mental illness was still viewed as a kind of degeneracy, and the picture was intended as a moral lesson warning against debauched behaviour.

Later in the eighteenth century the idea that people suffering mental distress needed humane care began to emerge. Public visiting to Bedlam was curtailed in 1770, although it continued in some form into the nineteenth century. The first-ever law to ensure the humane care of people with mental illness was passed in Tuscany in 1774, and in 1792 the first humane care for people with mental illness in the UK was provided by William Tuke, a quaker, who founded the York Retreat. Here patients were less restrained and confined, a healthy diet was provided and treatment included giving patients activities such as farm work (the beginnings of occupational therapy). Similarly, in 1794 Pinel introduced humane care at the asylum of La Bicêtre in Paris. He took the view that:

> The mentally sick, far from being guilty people deserving of punishment are sick people whose miserable state deserves all the consideration that is due to suffering humanity. One should try with the most simple methods to restore their reason. (cited in Tallis, 1998: 8)

Pinel in his *Medico-Philosophical Treatise on Mental Alienation or Mania* (1801) developed what he called 'traitement moral', which involved talking gently with the patient, offering warmth, and restoring hope – elements that research now demonstrates are central to effective psychotherapy.

The emergence of psychological diagnosis and treatment

In 1766 Franz Anton Mesmer published his ideas about what he called 'animal magnetism', seeking to account for mental disturbance as a result of physical forces. His 'animal magnetism' may best be understood as a kind of 'life force' and he conceived illness as an interruption of the natural flow of this 'subtle fluid'. His treatment system, known as mesmerism, was a precursor of hypnosis, which in turn influenced the development of psychological treatment and particularly psychoanalysis (Ellenberger, 1970).

During the nineteenth century the medicalisation of mental illness progressed as modern scientific medicine evolved. The idea that mental problems may have physical causes was supported by the development of microbiology (for example the connection between syphilis and the mental condition of 'general paresis'), establishing a trend of seeking physical and biological causes for emotional problems. This approach was reversed through the work of Charcot (1882) who, at the Salpêtrière hospital in Paris, began to look at psychological causes for physical symptoms. He believed he had identified a condition he called 'hystero-epilepsy', based on a group of patients who appeared to have both epileptic symptoms and 'hysteria'. It emerged that the epileptic convulsions were the result of suggestion and induction (hypnotism) due to the fact that these apparently 'hysteric' patients were placed on the same wards as the epileptics. Once these patients were separated from the epileptics, and their initial concerns (for example, distress, anxiety, family conflicts) were individually explored, their epileptic symptoms disappeared. Charcot developed treatment based on counter-suggestion to address what we would now call conversion disorders. The focus on the symptoms was redirected to looking at real-life concerns with a focus on solving these problems.

Sigmund Freud and psychoanalysis

Charcot's lectures and demonstrations of his new hypnotic treatment were attended by the young Sigmund Freud, around 1885. Freud, who had specialised in neurology, had begun to be interested in hypnotism and psychological treatment. Contact with Charcot further developed Freud's interest in psychology and the nature of neurosis which in turn led to his development of psychoanalytic theory and practice.

Sigmund Freud (1856–1939) emerged in the context of the nineteenth-century post-enlightenment preoccupation with the development of rationality and science. Religion, spirituality and romanticism were equally powerful aspects of his culture, however they were being scrutinised and questioned with a scientific eye. The publication of Darwin's *The Origin of Species* in 1859 represented an unprecedented upheaval in Western culture as beliefs about God and the nature of human beings were radically called into question. In focusing on human psychology, Freud was grappling with understanding scientifically the nature and workings of the human soul. Science was moving into the domain of human emotional and mental suffering, which had hitherto been configured in spiritual terms, as soul-sickness; and into the domain of healing, which had been the preserve of pastoral care.

Psychotherapy emerged as the child of religion and science, and Freud, as a doctor and as a Jew, held within himself the tensions of the relationship between these 'parents'. Although Freud was not a practising Jew, and indeed viewed religious belief as a form of neurosis (Linke, 1999) the religious/spiritual core of Judaism is inevitably a part of his heritage and its influence may be discerned in the evolution of psychotherapy. Given his medical training, Freud was concerned to establish the scientific credibility of psychological treatment, and specifically psychoanalytic theory. He faced the perennial problem of translating clinical experience with unique, individual patients into empirically valid theory and practice. The tension between the art of the healing relationship and scientific accountability is as evident in Freud's work as it is in current debates about the evidence base for psychotherapy.

So Freud sought to locate his theories in a medical model of sickness and treatment. Initially he collaborated with Breuer, using hypnotic techniques to work with patients who suffered with hysterical conversion symptoms. Freud's early theory (1895) was based on the case of 'Anna O', a patient of Breuer, and a number of women with similar difficulties (Freud and Breuer, 1895/1974). Anna O suffered from a range of physical symptoms for which no physical cause could be found, and also had mood swings and a form of hallucination. She named the treatment 'the talking cure' because it involved her entering a hypnotic state, in which she would speak about her symptoms and make links between specific symptoms and feelings, previous occurrences, and ultimately specific forgotten emotionally traumatic events from her past. Once these links were identified, the symptoms disappeared (Freud and Breuer, 1895/1974). The hypothesis was that traumatic events had been repressed into the unconscious mind, and the hysterical symptoms were signalling their presence. By retrieving and 'talking them away' the symptoms could be resolved. Later, instead of hypnosis, Freud developed the technique of 'free association', in which the patient lies on a couch and verbalises whatever thoughts come into their mind, without censoring or seeking logical connections. From these beginnings he developed key concepts including the role of the unconscious mind, the idea of defences, particularly repression and resistance, and the role of analysis or interpretation.

Freud's efforts to work within a scientific paradigm led him to seek 'objectivity' and this may lie behind his approach of making the therapist the neutral 'scientific instrument', the blank screen, which receives the productions of the patient: 'the physician should be opaque to the patient and, like a mirror, show nothing but what is shown to him' (in Tallis, 1998: 41).

The concept of the unconscious mind was also explored by other students of Charcot, notably Janet, whose *L'Automatisme psychologique* published in 1889 pre-dates Freud. However Freud developed this idea, formulating a cohesive (albeit complex and evolving) theory of the unconscious mind, and this is perhaps his greatest contribution, both to psychotherapeutic theory and to human culture and self-understanding. Freud formulated a theory of mental difficulty that accounted for overt mental (and sometimes physical) symptoms as being related to aspects of experience that have, because of their traumatic nature, been split off from conscious awareness and repressed so that they are held in the unconscious mind.

The idea that hysterical symptoms and neuroses had their roots in sexuality had existed since ancient times, when it was believed that they were caused by the movement of the uterus around the body. Although this view was discredited, many doctors, including Charcot and Breuer, held the view that sexuality was nevertheless in some way relevant for their patients. In the nineteenth century, female sexuality, if its existence was acknowledged at all, tended to be seen as unacceptable and problematic. Thus it was revolutionary for Freud to move away from the trauma theory described above and develop his theory of the role of libido (sex drive) in human psychological functioning. It was in keeping with the cultural norms of the time for Freud to hypothesise that psychopathology must arise from the repression of sexual needs and feelings.

Freud noted that many of his patients reported sexual experiences from childhood, and he initially took these to be factual memories. However he eventually abandoned this view and developed his theories of infantile sexuality and psychosexual development (1905). This theory was only slightly less shocking in his day than the idea that adults were sexually abusing children in their care. More recently Freud has been criticised for defining his patients' reports as fantasy and denying the possibility that real abuse might have taken place (e.g. Miller, 1981/1985).

Freud developed the notion of the pleasure principle – the drive for pleasurable sensation, and he focused specifically on sexual or sensual pleasure. He considered that, in normal development, the infant's pleasure focus was initially oral, that it then develops and shifts to an anal focus as the child gains control of bodily functions, and then to a phallic/genital focus at around three to six years of age. In relation to this he also identified what he called the Oedipal phase, in which the child's sexual focus is on the opposite gender parent, and reaches a crisis as the child, fearful of reprisal from the same gender parent, gives up and represses the sexual focus on the opposite gender parent. This repression is seen as part of normal development and enables the child to move into the next developmental phase, latency, and then to normal sexual maturity. Freud's theory was coloured by the gender perceptions of his day, and was much more clearly articulated in relation to male children than females.

His theory of psychopathology focused on the idea that for some reason the child gets stuck or fixated in her or his negotiation of the early developmental stages, so that the progress towards sexual maturity is interrupted and arrested. In adult life these unresolved fixations may emerge such that unacceptable infantile wishes and urges intrude into the adult consciousness. This generates anxiety and then a need to defend against both the anxiety and the infantile material, processes that may become evident as neurotic symptoms.

Much of Freud's work focused on treatment approaches, including the development of the analytic technique, and the exploration of dreams and of slips of the tongue, as ways to access the unconscious mind and address neurotic problems. He also developed the concepts of projection and transference fairly early on in his work, as he accounted for his patients' shows of affection and attraction toward him by seeing them as aspects of their past relationships emerging in the present. Later he focused on the transference process as a way to access unconscious material for analysis.

Freud and the therapeutic relationship

Much has been written about Freud's approach to the therapeutic relationship. The stereotypical image of Freudian analysis is of the patient lying on a couch, with the analyst out of sight behind them and saying little or nothing while the patient does the talking. The picture is of the analyst as a neutral 'blank screen' onto which the patient will project his or her experience of the 'other'. While it is true that Freudian psychoanalysts practise the 'rule of abstinence', meaning that they seek neutrality in their contact with the client, Freud, in his 1913 paper 'On beginning the treatment', highlights the importance of the therapist's 'sympathetic understanding' (1913: 140), and the importance of offering interpretations that are timely and well attuned to the client's level of insight and self-understanding. He also speaks of the crucial importance of establishing the patient's 'rapport' with the analyst and also of the patient's attachment to the treatment and to 'the person of the doctor' (Freud, 1913: 139). These statements are significant in that they indicate Freud's awareness that, in practice, the *relationship* is an essential aspect of successful treatment, even though he does not fully articulate this theoretically.

The dissemination of psychoanalytic ideas

Between 1910 and 1915 Freud surrounded himself with a group of students, including Jung, Adler, Rank, Reich and Ferenczi. Freud very much saw himself as pioneering a shift in human understanding and consciousness, that was as radical and far-reaching as the work of Galileo or Darwin. In this his style resembles the 'rabbinic mode' – perhaps an unconscious element from his Jewish cultural heritage. Freud shared his ideas dialogically with a small group of followers, much as a rabbi would, retaining a strong sense of his own authority and rightness. In Judaic tradition, this authority is handed down to followers who are committed to upholding the traditions, who become rabbis in their turn. This mode was a great strength in enabling the preservation of Jewish religion and culture. When translated into the establishment of psychoanalysis, it meant that it was difficult for members of Freud's circle to develop and add to Freud's theory, or revoke earlier ideas, without breaking away and forming a separate grouping. On the other hand, this approach ensured that psychoanalytic theory was established securely and clearly and has survived, both as theory and as practice up to the present day.

It could be argued that this model has profoundly influenced the evolution of psychotherapy. There is a tendency for schools of psychotherapeutic theory to be strongly identified with a single individual, although in fact the theory may often have been developed collaboratively. Furthermore, there has been a tendency until relatively recently for each theoretical school to be intent on ensuring its own survival through rigid and competitive differentiation from other approaches. This has militated against the identification of convergent therapeutic factors, and has also impeded the evolution of and recognition of pluralistic and integrative practice.

The first schism – departure of two key figures: Jung and Adler

Inevitably the members of Freud's circle began to develop their own theoretical ideas and to differentiate themselves from Freud. The first members of Freud's circle to break away were Jung and Adler.

Carl Gustav Jung (1875–1961) was Swiss, the son of a Protestant clergyman, and deeply interested in both the history of religion and the sciences. He trained in medicine and worked with severely psychotic patients. He was particularly concerned to articulate the links between the psychological and the spiritual, and to locate individual human experience within the universal. He sought to develop a holistic approach, which embraced both 'science' and 'soul'. This brought him into conflict with Freud, who wanted to secure a sound scientific reputation for psychoanalysis, and so Jung broke away from Freud in 1913 to develop the school of psychotherapy that became known as 'Analytical Psychology'.

Jung became interested in personality type and structure. He proposed that individuals have an outer 'persona', which hides the underlying aspects of personality, the 'shadow'. He believed that each person has masculine and feminine qualities – 'animus' and 'anima', and that for the individual to be healthy these need to be in balance. He identified extrovert and introvert personality types and also considered that it was important for the individual to balance thinking, feeling, intuition and sensuousness.

Perhaps his best-known contribution to psychological theory is his theory of archetypes. Where Freud recognised the patient's symbolism as individual and personal to him or herself, for Jung, symbols were overarching universal metaphors for human experience. These archetypal symbols, found in mythologies across many cultures, enabled Jung to develop his theory of the 'collective unconscious'. He proposed that alongside personal consciousness there exists a

> psychic system of a collective, universal, and impersonal nature which is identical in all individuals. This collective unconscious does not develop individually but is inherited. It consists of pre-existent forms, the archetypes ... (Jung, 1936/1959: 43)

Jung's theory, then, included a wider context – however, this was internal, psychological and spiritual, rather than social.

Alfred Adler (1870–1937), on the other hand, developed his theory to emphasise the role of family and social relationships in the development of psychological problems. Adler was born in Vienna and became a doctor. He developed the idea that human beings must be considered as unique individuals in the context of their environment. In this he diverged from Freud's theories based on drives and instincts. Despite these differences he became part of Freud's circle in 1902, although his divergence from Freud led to Adler's departure in 1911, to develop his own psychological theories.

Adler developed an 'integrated, holistic theory of human nature and psychopathology, a set of principles and techniques of psychotherapy, a world view, and a philosophy of living' that represented 'a vigorously optimistic, humanistic view of life' (Stein and Edwards, 1998: 67).

He believed in an innate growth-oriented life-force, and emphasised both the uniqueness of the individual, and the indivisibility of the individual from his or her context of cultural inheritance and community. Thus he considered that a sense of community (*Gemeinshaftsgefeuhl*) was essential to mental health. He believed that the child's early responses to the family community became a 'prototype' for that person's approach to life, and believed the individual consciously or unconsciously directs his or her own existence. His treatment approach reflected his philosophical differences from traditional psychoanalysis, in being more dialogic, and focusing on changing beliefs, behaviours and feelings with the goal of replacing 'exaggerated self-protection, self-enhancement, and self-indulgence with courageous social contribution' (Stein, 2003: Appx 1).

Adler's perspective was to have a crucial impact on the development of psychotherapeutic theory and in particular the emergence of the humanistic psychotherapies. Furthermore, his interest in social context resulted in him playing a pioneering role in the development of the child guidance movement.

Further departures from Freud

Sándor Ferenczi (1873–1933) was born in Hungary, became a doctor, and met Freud in 1908 (Hoffman, 2003). However, he challenged the Freudian technique of analytic neutrality, which he saw as inimical to psychological healing, and potentially a form of sadistic mistreatment of patients (Maccoby, 1995). Ferenczi's key contribution was in his understanding of the therapeutic relationship. He proposed (1928) that the analyst should be active, authentic and convey warmth, viewing the patient as an equal partner in the therapeutic process. He saw this relationship as a crucial factor in enabling the patient to 'establish ... the contrast between the present and the unbearable traumatogenic past' (Ferenczi, 1933: 160 in Hoffman, 2003).

Ferenczi was an early exponent of the role of empathy and emotional attunement in the therapeutic process:

> I have come to the conclusion that it is above all a question of psychological tact whether one should tell the patient some particular thing. But what is 'tact'? It is the capacity for empathy. (Ferenczi, 1928: 89 in Hoffman, 2003)

He believed the analyst should 'use feelings and intuitions as tools, to analyze with heart and libido as well as with intellect' (Maccoby, 1995). He also recommended that psychoanalysts must undergo personal analysis in order to become emotionally self-aware, and that then they could monitor their internal responses (countertransference), seeing this as a resource for understanding the patient. He articulated a core idea that is now central to most psychotherapeutic theories.

Another key figure was Otto Rank (1884–1939) who developed an important new theory focusing on the real mother–child relationship, examining the role of the birth experience and the separation from mother in the development of anxiety. He was interested in briefer forms of therapy and in the importance of the real here-and-now relationship in psychotherapy. His work with Ferenczi exploring the nature of the therapeutic relationship culminated in the publication in 1924 of a ground-breaking monograph: *The Development of Psychoanalysis* (Ferenczi and Rank, 1925/1986). Rank visited the US several times before emigrating permanently in 1935. There his work was influential in the emerging American humanistic and existential psychotherapies.

Following Rank and Ferenczi's work highlighting the interpersonal contact between analyst and patient, Franz Alexander (1891–1964), a Hungarian 'second generation' psychoanalyst, developed these ideas further. He had some contact with Freud, but moved to the University of Chicago. He is perhaps best known for his highly controversial theory, published in 1946, that the primary curative factor in psychotherapy is the emotional relationship with the analyst, rather than intellectual insight. He considered that the analyst should purposely provide a 'corrective emotional experience' in the transference relationship in order to repair the patient's past traumatic relational experiences (Alexander and French, 1946). He acknowledged the influence of Ferenczi in stressing the importance of the therapeutic relationship, and his ideas prefigure those of Kohut's self-psychology and of current humanistic and integrative theories of developmentally needed relationship as an aspect of psychotherapy (e.g. Clarkson, 1992; Erskine, 1993).

Sullivan's interpersonal theory

Another key exponent of the role and importance of the interpersonal was Harry Stack Sullivan (1892–1949), an American psychiatrist who did pioneering work with schizophrenics and became a psychoanalyst in the 1930s in New York. He gradually moved away from Freudian intrapsychic theories to develop a relationally based theory of personality development. Like Rank, Sullivan viewed the relationship between mother and infant as central to healthy psychological development, addressing both biological needs and also the basic need for security. He thought that early relational security, and 'the mothering one's' own ability to manage her anxiety and convey empathy resulted in the child developing a sense of 'interpersonal security'. Furthermore he considered that 'the tension of anxiety, when present in the mothering one, induces anxiety in the infant' (Sullivan, 1953: 41). His ideas underpin the emergence of 'Interpersonal Psychoanalysis' and 'Interpersonal Psychotherapy' as a body of theory and practice.

These early theorists had a significant influence on the broader development of psychotherapy. Meanwhile the psychoanalytic strand of psychotherapeutic theory continued to develop both in Europe and in the United States. There is not sufficient space here to discuss the many significant contributions to psychoanalytic theory by the 'neo-Freudians' such as Horney, Thompson and Fromm, or the evolution of psychoanalysis in France by theorists such as Lacan.

British developments in psychoanalysis

In England, traditional Freudian ideas were carried forward by Ernest Jones (who founded The London Psychoanalytical Society in 1913) and Anna Freud. Anna Freud made major theoretical contributions to the development of ego psychology, seeing the ego as developing defence mechanisms to protect from the anxiety resulting from both intrapsychic and external reality-based threats. Thus, while she maintained Sigmund Freud's theories of drive and instinct as central, she did also include external context as a factor.

Her other major contribution was in the development of psychoanalytic work with children during and after the Second World War.

The emergence of object relations theory

A key development that emerged in England was the development of object relations theory. The historical roots of this development go back to Ferenczi's ideas, and were developed initially by Melanie Klein (1882–1960) and later by Fairbairn, Winnicott and Guntrip (the so-called 'English School').

Klein, writing in 1935, focused on the very early phases of child development, revising Freud's views and formulating the idea that the infant, unable to experience self and other as distinct, identifies 'part objects', which are imbued with 'good' and 'bad' qualities according to whether they are a source of pleasure or pain. The infant is not able to experience both good and bad as aspects of the same person, whether self or other, and so splits them from each other, experiencing pleasurable union with the 'good' and terror of annihilation by the 'bad'. Klein called this early developmental phase the 'paranoid–schizoid position'. She believed that the infant copes with the threat of the 'bad' by means of primitive defensive operations such as idealisation, projection and projective identification. In normal development the splitting of good and bad gradually reduces and the infant is able to perceive self and other as whole 'objects' integrating good and bad. This Klein called 'the depressive position'. In recognising that he/she both loves and hates one person the infant becomes anxious that his/her own hate could result in loss of the object, and develops the capacity for reparation through the expression of love. Where this process becomes derailed, the child is likely to mature without having integrated good and bad, and thus continue to resort to the primitive defences described above.

Klein focused on the early intrapsychic experience of the patient, and did not include real-life factors in her analysis. Like Anna Freud, Klein pioneered psychotherapeutic work with children. Key contributions were her recognition of the role of play as a means to access the child's inner world, and her work with very young children, whom she believed could make use of theoretically based interpretations of their symbolic play. Klein's theory and approach both with adults and children were considered highly controversial. However, it established the central significance of the mother–infant relationship in the psychological development of the child, which became a cornerstone of the British object relations school.

William Fairbairn departed radically from Freudian theory when he proposed that 'libido is object seeking, not pleasure seeking' (1952: 127). He thought that the infant internalised the 'other' to form an internal 'object' which becomes part of the child's psychological structure. The other is not fully assimilated, but is capable of being differentiated and experienced as, for example, 'mother's voice' expressing views, rules and so on. The person may then act as though mother were indeed present, perhaps encouraging, perhaps criticising or prohibiting. Fairbairn identified developmental stages that must be negotiated, moving through phases of dependence to a mature more 'separate' relationship to the other (Eagle and Wolitsky, 1992). The therapeutic emphasis was on the interpretation of problems in terms of early relationships and development. Fairbairn, like Alexander, viewed the therapeutic relationship as a primary source of psychological repair, serving as a means to replace the internal 'bad object' with a 'good object' – the internalised therapist.

This idea was developed further by Donald Winnicott (1958/1992) and Guntrip (1969/1992). They both developed the idea of regression to the point when normal development went 'wrong', seeing psychotherapy as the provision of a reparative relationship enabling a more healthy forward development. For Winnicott, the 'holding' provided by the psychotherapist was a reality which gave troubled patients a novel experience of what he called 'good enough' mothering, which had been missing in their early experience. This is a clear articulation of the use of the therapeutic relationship to address developmental deficits directly, and contrasts sharply with traditional psychoanalytic theory.

Much of Winnicott's work focused on therapeutic work with children, and he powerfully evoked the loving bond that exists in a healthy infant–mother relationship, along with the traumas and terrors infants experience when this relationship is ruptured or deficient.

Influence of Bowlby and developmental psychology

These ideas were given a scientific underpinning by John Bowlby, whose studies in developmental psychology resulted in the development of attachment theory in the 1940s and 1950s (Bowlby, 1969/1989). Bowlby had studied both medicine and psychoanalysis and had a questioning, scientific, open-minded approach.

Where psychoanalytic theory took the view that the whole object relation is constructed in the child's fantasy and is based in innate drives, Bowlby proposed that pathology is a result not of unresolved fantasies but of pathogenic environmental factors. At the Tavistock Clinic in London he and colleagues demonstrated this through their research and through film evidence of the effects of separation on small children (Robertson and Robertson, 1969). Bowlby developed the theory that infants have an innate drive for attachment, and a need for affectional bonds. He saw attachment as having survival value as it ensured security and protection from danger, especially when the child is tired, sick or frightened.

Attachment behaviour is any form of behaviour that results in a person attaining or maintaining proximity to some other clearly identified individual who is conceived as better able to cope with the world. (Bowlby, 1988: 26–7)

While attachment is most obvious in children, Bowlby recognised that 'attachment behaviour is held to characterize human beings from the cradle to the grave' (Bowlby, 1994: 129). So for Bowlby the actual early relationship, provided it is adequately responsive to the child's needs, is the source of secure internal object relations. The child develops a secure 'internal working model' (Bowlby, 1988) which becomes a template for secure relating throughout life. Similarly early insecure attachment experience creates a template that results in an ongoing pattern of insecure relating. Bowlby's theory presented a major challenge to the psychoanalytic world and was only slowly accepted into object relations theory. Today it is a central element of much psychotherapeutic theory and practice, and recent scientific breakthroughs in neuropsychobiology (Schore, 2003) are providing new information that supports and develops Bowlby's ideas.

Heinz Kohut and self-psychology

Perhaps one of the most significant of the more recent developments within psychoanalytic theory has been Kohut's self-psychology (Kohut, 1971, 1984). Kohut's ideas emerged from his clinical experience with people who had a profoundly fragmented sense of self (Siegel, 1996). He identified the importance of the early relationships in the building of 'self-structure'. The child experiences self-functions (for example soothing, emotional regulation) as being performed for him/her by the other or 'selfobject'. Gradually these functions are internalised and the child experiences that during manageable absences of the other she or he can now perform these functions for him or herself. Failures of the 'selfobject' at different phases of early development result in psychological deficits in the person's sense of self. Kohut recognised that clients with these difficulties demanded in the transferential relationship that the therapist act as a selfobject, and he saw the therapeutic task as offering empathic interpretations that enable the client to internalise these missing selfobject functions more adequately. He called this process 'transmuting internalisation' (Kohut, 1984). Kohut's work, developed in America, was highly controversial in its time, although his theoretical ideas can be seen to correspond with some aspects of British object relations theory (Milton et al., 2004). His work has done much, through his understanding of the significance of empathic attunement, to establish a continuum between psychodynamic and humanistic approaches.

Emergence of behavioural and cognitive therapies

Alongside the development of psychoanalytic psychotherapy with its focus on instinctual drives, early experience and unconscious processes, a very different paradigm for psychotherapy was emerging. This approach grew from advances in behavioural science, learning theory, cognitive psychology and experimental psychology between 1910 and 1920 (Fishman and Franks, 1992). It encompasses a range of therapies including behaviour therapy, cognitive therapy, cognitive-behavioural therapy and rational emotive behaviour therapy. Broadly defined these approaches seek to use evidence-based techniques with the goal of producing constructive change in cognitions and/or behaviour that solve the presenting problem.

Learning theories

The basis for these therapies is in the behavioural learning theories developed by Watson, Pavlov and Skinner. John Watson (1878–1958) developed behaviour theory and in 1913 defined psychology as 'a purely objective experimental branch of natural science. Its theoretical goal is the prediction and control of *behaviour* [*sic*]' (Watson, 1913: 158).

These psychologists conducted experiments with animals that demonstrated that behaviour can be manipulated. Ivan P. Pavlov (1849–1936) demonstrated in 1903 that the reflex of a dog to salivate in the presence of food, can be 'conditioned' so that if a bell is rung at the same moment, eventually the dog will salivate when a bell is rung and no food is present (Lovell, 2000). This became known as 'classical conditioning' of behaviour. In 1938 B.F. Skinner (1904–1990), published his research demonstrating that a specific behaviour could be increased or reduced depending on the immediate consequence of that behaviour (operant conditioning). These consequences are known as 'reinforcers' and may be positive (presence of reward) or negative (absence of reward) (Skinner, 1938/1999).

Conditioning and behaviour therapy

In the UK, Hans Eysenck, a psychiatrist, had become disillusioned with traditional psychoanalytic approaches and in his 1952 study he attempted to discredit psychotherapy. This critique of the scientific basis for psychoanalysis led him to explore and research behavioural techniques at the Institute of Psychiatry at the Maudsley Hospital in London (Eysenck, 1959), and he was one of the first to use the term 'behaviour therapy'. The focus for Eysenck and his colleagues was on applying learning theory and conditioning techniques to treat psychiatric problems, enabling the patient to develop more adaptive behaviours.

Early critics of behaviour therapy, and particularly of 'operant conditioning', were concerned that a therapy designed to change behaviour could be used to gain social and political control. B.F. Skinner's *Walden Two* (1948) is a Utopian vision of social manipulation of human behaviour – however it is evident that the same techniques could be misused for political ends. It is perhaps because early work in this field emerged from psychiatry and was conducted with mentally ill or learning disabled people, including children, that concerns about consent became a focus. Fishman and Franks (1992) therefore make the point that therapeutic change should be considered desirable and ethical by the patient as well as those around him or her.

Joseph Wolpe and Arnold Lazarus

Another early pioneer of behaviour therapy was Wolpe, a South African, who in 1958 developed the intervention of systematic desensitisation as a way to treat phobias. This involved exposing the patient to a manageable level of the fear stimulus, until the fear response subsided. The level of exposure was gradually increased until the patient could tolerate full exposure without an associated fear response (Tallis, 1998). These ideas were developed further by Arnold Lazarus, who studied with Wolpe. He used Wolpe's methods of systematic desensitisation, along with existing psychotherapeutic methods of support and insight, to develop a therapy that could be used to treat a range of psychological problems (Fishman and Franks, 1992). Lazarus is also credited with being one of the first to use the term 'behaviour therapy' to describe his approach (Lazarus, 1958), and he certainly played a major role in the further development and establishment of the behavioural psychotherapies when he and Wolpe moved to the United States.

In the 1960s and 1970s behavioural therapies became well researched and well established. As well as the exposure techniques such as that described above, interventions included the modelling of the desired behaviour, training and coaching in social skills, and the use of self-help strategies (Glass and Arnkoff, 1995). Neither Eysenck nor Wolpe considered the therapeutic relationship to be a curative factor in itself, and initially it was very much downplayed in order to highlight the contrast with psychoanalytic models. More recently the presence of a supportive relationship has been acknowledged as significant to positive outcomes.

In the later 1970s it gradually became clear that while research showed behaviour therapy to be effective for symptom relief in many anxiety-based behavioural problems (such as phobias), it had more limited success with problems (such as depression) where non-observable, internal processes are significant. This was a key factor in the emergence of the cognitive therapies.

Cognitive therapies: Albert Ellis and Aaron Beck

In the mid-1950s there was an upsurge of interest in cognition within the field of experimental psychology, known as the 'cognitive revolution' (Murray, 1995). Among clinicians there was a growing interest in the role played by cognition in the formation and maintenance of human difficulties. In the 1950s both Albert Ellis and Aaron Beck, who were practising psychoanalysts, were beginning to explore this area. Ellis developed 'rational therapy' in 1955 (Dryden, 2000), publishing *Reason and Emotion in Psychotherapy* in 1962. Ellis developed his ABC model, which proposed the idea that Activating events in a person's life results in painful emotional Consequences (depression, distress) because of the internal irrational Beliefs the person holds in relation to the event. Ellis intervened directly to challenge and alter these beliefs, resulting in the person feeling and functioning better. Early on Ellis' approach became known as rational-emotive therapy, and in 1993 it was renamed 'rational emotive behaviour therapy', to acknowledge its behavioural as well as its cognitive and emotional aspects.

Aaron Beck first published his theories of cognitive therapy in the 1960s. Initially both behavioural and psychoanalytic psychotherapists roundly rejected them. However, with the publication of *Cognitive Therapy and the Emotional Disorders* (Beck, 1976/1991), cognitive psychotherapy began to gain recognition and respect. Beck proposed that our cognitions affect our feelings, behaviour and physical responses. Throughout life we develop cognitive 'schemas' or templates, based on past experience, which in turn lead to selective perception and evaluation of stimuli that reinforce the schema. These schemas may be helpful or dysfunctional. Because cognitions are conscious we can access them and change them, thus interrupting the schema, and the thinking processes that maintain it, and this can then lead to changes in feelings and behaviours.

For Beck, the role of the therapist is to form a collaborative, problem-solving alliance with the client, and treatment involves teaching theory and challenging cognitive 'errors' in order to develop more helpful cognitions and schemas. Treatment also involves behavioural interventions, the purpose of these being to alter cognitions. As with behaviour therapy, the relationship itself is not considered a key factor in therapeutic change, although a good working alliance is considered essential.

Further developments in cognitive and behavioural therapy

Another key figure in the development of the cognitive therapies was Donald Meichenbaum, who, as well as making important contributions to theory, played an important role in promoting the professional acceptance of the cognitive therapies by, in 1975, establishing the 'Cognitive-Behavior Modification Newsletter' (Arnkoff and Glass, 1995). This was a significant factor in avoiding a theory-driven split, and cognitive approaches have been integrated by a majority of behaviour therapists, who now consider themselves 'cognitive behavioural' therapists.

Many of the key developments in cognitive and cognitive-behavioural approaches in psychotherapy have taken place in the United States. These therapies, however, are well recognised and used worldwide. The British Association for Behavioural Psychotherapy founded in 1972 was the focus of developments in the UK, and in 1993 it changed its name to The British Association for Behavioural and Cognitive Psychotherapists to reflect the growing integration of cognitive and behavioural approaches (Lomas, 1985/2005). Partly because they are rooted in the empirical paradigm shared by natural science and medicine (Fishman and Franks, 1992) these approaches have evolved an extensive evidence base, which has facilitated their acceptance within mainstream mental health provision.

A more recent advance in cognitive and behavioural psychotherapy takes account of the relative nature of experience, rather than assuming that there is an objective, rational 'truth' that a client can be taught to recognise (e.g. Guidano and Liotti, 1983; Neimeyer, 1986; Mahoney, 1990). These 'constructivist cognitive therapies' share many theoretical and technical elements with modern psychodynamic and humanistic approaches (Arnkoff and Glass, 1995: 669), and perhaps represent a move from the cognitive field towards psychotherapy integration.

The development of the humanistic psychotherapies

Although the humanistic psychotherapies are often stereotyped as a rebelling 'Third Force', emerging in the 1960s as a reaction against the 'old guard' of psychoanalysis and behaviour therapy, in fact it is probably more realistic to see them as one of many developments and evolutions, with strong roots in psychodynamic theory. As we have seen, the history of psychoanalysis and psychodynamic psychotherapy has involved many divergences and developments that, in their day, were as radical as the development of the humanistic psychotherapies. Key ideas such as the role of real experience in the development of psychological problems, and the curative importance of the actual here-and-now contact between therapist and client, were identified as significant by these psychoanalysts. These clinical ideas, together with a number of philosophical principles, are the defining features across the whole range of humanistic therapies.

Philosophical aspects of the humanistic psychotherapies

HUMAN POTENTIAL AND FREEDOM Humanistic psychotherapists generally share an optimistic view of human beings, recognising that people have a 'life-force' that moves them towards health and well-being, rejecting the view that people are innately 'bad' or 'flawed'. While recognising that people can be extremely troubled and seemingly self-destructive, the humanistic view is that people have freedom and responsibility to choose how they create their lives and they can be enabled to find their own internal resources even in very adverse circumstances. This is sometimes misunderstood as ignoring genetic endowment, or life circumstances, or as promoting unrealistic omnipotence. In fact it is more a recognition that people can find self-worth and dignity, despite the limitations they meet.

HOLISM People are seen as indivisible from their context and indivisible in themselves, an idea drawn from Kurt Lewin's field theory (Parlett, 1991). So for the humanistic psychotherapist, the individual is unique and cannot be separated into, for example, mind and body, or thinking and feeling. The person is a unity of mind, body, action, feelings and spirit. Every aspect of the person is contingent upon every other aspect and cannot be separated off. Equally, the person's context (life situation, culture) cannot be ignored without inevitably misunderstanding or misperceiving the person.

RELATIONSHIP Another core value is the centrality of human relatedness. Human beings are viewed as essentially social, and there is a recognition that problems often have their source in human relating, and that the human relationship offered by the psychotherapist is the most potent healing aspect in the psychotherapeutic process. Clearly these ideas exist in other psychotherapeutic theories (e.g. Bowlby, Kohut) – however the humanistic psychotherapies played a significant role in defining the therapeutic relationship itself as a central source of resolution and healing (Rogers, 1951/1990).

PHENOMENOLOGY The humanistically based psychotherapist is interested in meeting the client's experience without bringing personal or theoretical assumptions that might cause them to pre-judge the client's difficulties or their causes. By encouraging the client to pay attention to all aspects of his or her experience equally, new meaning and significance can emerge.

While each of these values is by no means unique to the humanistic psychotherapies, the constellation of them, taken together, and their centrality in defining the humanistic paradigm is what gives these approaches a common ground and also what differentiates them from the other major 'schools' of psychotherapy. Perhaps it is because many of the principles of humanistic psychotherapy derive from philosophical values, and include the spiritual dimension of human experience, that these therapies have emerged so strongly over the past 50 years, gaining wide recognition and acceptance with clients. It is perhaps also for this reason that the development of a research evidence base for the humanistic psychotherapies has been a particular challenge.

Early forerunners: Jaspers and Buber

As psychoanalysis was developing, the philosophy of existentialism, which emerged in nineteenth-century Europe, was beginning to influence the field of psychiatry (van Deurzen-Smith, 1997). In 1913, Karl Jaspers, a German psychiatrist and philosopher, was incorporating existential ideas from contemporary philosophers into an approach to human suffering and healing. In 1913 he published *Allgemeine Psychopathologie* (*General Psychopathology*) in which he explored the psychological significance of these ideas. He identifies the role of phenomenological observation, and is perhaps the first to recognise the importance of 'empathic understanding' (Einfühlen), in enabling us to connect with and understand the inner world of the patient: 'We sink ourselves into the psychic situation and *understand genetically by empathy* [*sic*] how one psychic event emerges from another' (Jaspers, 1913/1959: 301).

Thus Jaspers identifies the importance of human relatedness, seeing it as an essential human need and a key therapeutic tool. In Jaspers' work we thus find perhaps the earliest exploration of some of the ideas underpinning humanistic psychotherapy.

In the 1920s the centrality of human relatedness was further articulated by Martin Buber, a philosopher who had a major influence on the development of existential psychotherapy, and also Gestalt therapy. Buber proposed that human existence is essentially dialogical and that we only exist in relation to the other. He identified two modes of relating, both of which are essential to life: the contactful and authentic 'I–thou' relationship, and the practical, goal-directed 'I–it' relationship (Buber, 1923/2004).

Carl Rogers and person-centred psychotherapy

Humanistic psychotherapy became more established through Rogers' work in the United States from the 1930s onward. Both Adler and Rank were involved in the child guidance movement at that time, and it is within this field, and influenced by Rank (Cain and Seeman, 2001), that Rogers began to develop his 'Client-centred therapy'. Rogers believed that people 'have within themselves sufficient drive towards health' (Kirschenbaum, 1979: 75), which may be thwarted by life experiences, but that, given the right conditions, the person will find within themselves the capacity to move forward and resolve difficulties.

Rogers' landmark presentation on 'Newer Concepts in Psychotherapy', given at the University of Minnesota in 1940 (Cain and Seeman, 2001) critiqued existing psychotherapeutic approaches, and offered a radical new perspective. At the core of Rogers' approach is the idea that the provision of a respectful, empathic and authentic relationship will in itself enable the client to activate his or her capacity for 'responsible self-direction' (Rogers, 1951/1990: 64) in solving his or her own problems. Rogers' core conditions of 'empathic understanding', 'acceptance' and 'genuineness' (Rogers, 1961/1989: 61–2) have become central to most humanistic psychotherapies, and are increasingly becoming integrated into other approaches.

Rogers' theory and clinical practice has often been perceived as 'intuitive' or as little more than a set of beliefs or a philosophy, and this belies the clinical rigour of his work. Throughout his career Rogers was committed to the rigorous observation and evaluation of his ideas in clinical practice, and his work represents some of the earliest systematic research into psychotherapy (Cain and Seeman, 2001).

Rogers and Buber

In 1957 Rogers and Buber explored their ideas through a theoretical dialogue. Rogers particularly resonated with Buber's notion of 'confirming the other', by which Buber meant confirming the client's positive potentialities. However Rogers saw in this an implicit non-acceptance of 'negative' aspects of the client, which, for Rogers, was a form of judgement and objectification which undermines the client's 'self-actualising tendency' and is inimical to the principles of person-centred psychotherapy.

Existential psychotherapy

Existential psychotherapy has its roots in the philosophical ideas of Kierkegaard (1813–1855), Nietzsche (1844–1900), Heidegger (1889–1976), Husserl (1859–1938), Merleau-Ponty (1907–1961), Sartre (1905–1980) and Tillich (1886–1965) (van Deurzen-Smith, 1997).

As early as 1908 the psychiatrist J.L. Moreno was drawing on existential ideas of personal responsibility in his use of drama techniques in psychotherapeutic groups to enable patients to process early family difficulties and conflicts (Clarkson, 1992). As we have seen, Buber was also a key figure in the development of existential psychotherapy. Another significant contribution came from Viktor Frankl, who from his experience in the Nazi concentration camps developed 'logotherapy' (Frankl, 1946/2004), an existentially based psychotherapeutic approach focusing on the 'search for meaning' as the key to psychological survival and well-being. Frankl proposes that the focus in psychotherapy must be on the here-and-now and on life to come, rather than on early experience, and that owning freedom of will and finding meaning in life are central to psychological health.

In the UK Ronald Laing (1927–1989) was strongly influenced by existentialism in the development of the 'anti-psychiatry' movement, which sought to address psychotic disturbances such as schizophrenia without the use of medication to interfere with the patient's self-experience. He considered that psychotic experiences could be understood as 'an extreme form of existential misery' (van Deurzen-Smith, 1997: 163), and could be amenable to psychotherapeutic help. Also working in the UK, Emmy van Deurzen has done much to develop existential psychotherapy, and in the United States, Rollo May and Irvin Yalom have made significant contributions.

Gestalt therapy

Gestalt is a word derived from the German – it means whole, form, shape, body, framework. Gestalt therapy was originated by Fritz Perls and his wife Laura. Perls became a neuropsychiatrist, and briefly had analysis with Karen Horney, following which he trained as a psychoanalyst himself and worked in Berlin. During the 1920s he came into contact with gestalt psychology and existentialism. In 1933 he fled from fascism in Germany and moved to South Africa, where he founded the psychoanalytic society (1936). He began to develop his own ideas, departing from traditional psychoanalytic theory, but they were not well received. He moved to the US and in 1947, with Laura, began the first therapy group from which emerged gestalt therapy. In 1951 *Gestalt Therapy: Excitement and Growth in the Human Personality* (Perls et al., 1951/1990) was published.

The goals of gestalt therapy are based in phenomenology, focusing on raising awareness, enlarging choice and facilitating the client to make full contact with themselves and the environment. There is no focus on change or problem solving; rather the view is that by focusing on 'what is', the client inevitably becomes aware of alternatives, which he or she is then free to choose (Beisser, 1970). Here we can see the humanistic principle that human beings are self-regulating organisms with an inbuilt movement towards development and the meeting of present needs. Change is inevitable because it is the normal, natural state of affairs when a person is in contact with him or herself and their environment. When contact is interrupted the person becomes unable to meet his or her needs. This may happen in early life, resulting in what gestalt therapists call 'unfinished business' – repetitive patterned interruptions to their 'organismic flow'. Addressing these interruptions is the primary focus of gestalt therapy, and this is done by paying attention to and exploring current experience.

For Perls the therapist acted as a facilitator, and the focus was on the client's phenomenological world, rather than on the relationship with the therapist. He emphasised self-support, challenging the client who looked to the therapist to provide any external support. Having rejected the alienated relationship of traditional psychoanalysis, Perls appeared to have arrived at another kind of alienation, based on existential aloneness.

Gestalt theory since Perls has developed to incorporate the concept of the dialogic relationship from Buber's work (Richard Hycner, 1985; Lynne Jacobs, 1989), and current gestalt therapeutic practice thus emphasises that phenomenological exploration takes place through the medium of the dialogic relationship between therapist and client (Yontef, 1993).

Another recent development has been a move towards the integration of psychodynamic and self-psychology theories with Gestalt therapy (e.g. Hycner and Jacobs, 1995).

Other humanistic approaches

The emergence of the humanistic psychotherapies gained momentum after the Second World War, and it became clear that many different theories were emerging. Moreno's early work described above evolved into modern psychodrama, body-focused humanistic psychotherapies have emerged from Wilhelm Reich's work, while the transpersonal psychotherapies, including psychosynthesis, have explored the domain of human soul and spirit (e.g. Rowan, 1993; Wellings and McCormick, 2000).

The personal as political: equality and oppression

It is within the humanistic psychotherapies that perhaps most attention has been paid to issues of equality and oppression. Carl Rogers was very interested in the political power of personal change (Rogers, 1978). The women's movement in the 1960s and 1970s coined the phrase 'the personal is political' and focused on raising self-awareness (consciousness-raising) as a political tool. In 1981, feminist therapists Sheila Ernst and Lucy Goodison published *In Our Own Hands: A Book of Self-help Therapy* which sought to wrest psychotherapy from the hands of 'the experts' and make it accessible to women. Feminist therapy has since developed into a therapeutic model in its own right, across humanistic and psychodynamic fields. It seeks to challenge the patriarchal assumptions that are seen to be inherent in most psychotherapeutic approaches and to empower women to develop their self-esteem, assertiveness and capacity to author their own lives (McLellan, 1995). Similarly the 'pink therapy' movement (Davies and Charles, 1996) focuses on psychotherapy with lesbian, gay and bisexual clients.

Undoubtedly the humanistic psychotherapy movement represents a rich diversity of psychotherapeutic theory and practice that seeks to address the full range of human experience. It is characterised by openness and flexibility to explore and widen the horizons of psychotherapy; however this has at times been viewed as a dilution and oversimplification of the complex task of addressing human distress. John Rowan in *The Reality Game* (1983), gave a comprehensive critical overview of the humanistic psychotherapy movement in Britain in the early 1980s, recognising both its strengths and its shortcomings.

Psychotherapy integration

The evolution of psychotherapy has been characterised by the emergence of widely differing theories, often associated with key figures or founders of the approach in question. Alongside this process of forging new theory, since as early as 1936 (Rosenzweig, 1936), there has been an interest in the bringing together of different psychotherapeutic approaches. Arkowitz (1991, 1992) in the first volume of the *Journal of Psychotherapy Integration*, identifies three kinds of integration: theoretical integration, which has primarily focused on the integration of psychodynamic and behavioural psychotherapy theory (Dollard and Miller, 1950; Wachtel, 1977); the 'common factors approach', involving the identification across the range of psychotherapies of common factors that are 'most strongly associated with positive therapeutic outcome' (Arkowitz, 1992: 275); and technical eclecticism, which is based on a pragmatic, atheoretical attempt to identify the psychotherapeutic techniques most suited to particular presenting problems (for example Lazarus' Multimodal Therapy (Lazarus, 1967)).

In 1997 Arkowitz revisited his classification of psychotherapy integration, commenting that recent developments showed that 'theoretical integration is not so integrative, common factors not so common, and systematic eclecticism is not so eclectic' (Arkowitz,

1997: 258). According to Messer (1992), most theoretical integration involves a core theoretical model into which aspects of other theories are assimilated, rather than an equalised merging of two distinct models. He called this process 'assimilative integration'. An example of this integration is Linehan's 'dialectical behaviour therapy' (1993), which was developed to treat severe, self-harming borderline personality disordered people. In Linehan's approach elements of Zen philosophy are incorporated into an essentially cognitive-behavioural model.

Stricker (1994) points out that most approaches that have been viewed as examples of 'technical eclecticism', are in fact rooted in an identifiable theoretical framework, and thus would be better described as forms of 'assimilative integration'. This is exemplified in Holmes and Bateman (2002), where a number of chapters present integrative therapy viewed from different 'core' theoretical perspectives.

Arkowitz (1997) critiques the 'common factors' approach, suggesting that it is not clearly proven that such factors are indeed truly universal and uniform as the effective element across all therapies because research is not able to take full account of the limitless variables inherent in psychotherapeutic work. Holmes and Bateman (2002), however, consider the case for the existence of 'common factors' to be convincing, especially regarding the 'therapeutic alliance'. A related more recent perspective is the identification of integrating principles or foci, such as the therapeutic relationship (Barr, 1987; Clarkson, 1995) or the 'self' (Greenberg et al., 1993; Wolfe, 1995).

Holmes and Bateman (2002) critique the impact of evidence-based practice on the development of psychotherapy integration. They recognise that much integration occurs through flexible clinical practice by experienced and skilled psychotherapists faced with the particular needs of a specific client. The need for consistent 'manualised' psychotherapy approaches that lend themselves to replicable research studies precludes the exploration of flexible, integration strategies, resulting in a very limited evidence base for the integrative psychotherapies. Only where a specifically integrative model has been developed (for example Cognitive Analytic Therapy – Ryle, 1982) is the development of an evidence base straightforward.

Arkowitz's (1997) account draws primarily on psychotherapy research findings, and this limits his perspective. In particular he identifies very few examples of psychotherapy integration involving the humanistic psychotherapies. In fact integration has been a theme within the humanistic psychotherapies for many years. As we have seen, many are effectively an integration of theories and techniques from a variety of sources. An example of a humanistically based integrative approach is Transactional Analysis. This approach is variously regarded as psychodynamic (Tallis, 1998) and as humanistic (Feltham and Horton, 2000) and also includes an integration of cognitive and behavioural theory and technique.

Transactional Analysis (TA)

Developed in the 1950s and 1960s in the United States by Eric Berne, a Canadian doctor and psychoanalyst, TA is rooted in the humanistic and existential values. Its core theory, the ego-state model, is a sophisticated model of intrapsychic structure and psychodynamics evolved from psychoanalysis (Berne, 1961/2001). Berne also drew on learning theory and concepts of 'reinforcement' in developing his ideas about repetitive self-defeating strategies that maintain the person's 'life script' (Clarkson, 1992). Since Berne, TA, while maintaining its own distinct identity, has incorporated theory and technique from diverse sources, examples being the integration of techniques from gestalt therapy (Goulding and Goulding, 1979), or of self-psychology theory and neuroscientific findings (Hargaden and Sills, 2002). There is considerable justification therefore for regarding it as an early and evolving example of 'assimilative integration' (Arkowitz, 1997).

Recent publications in the UK (Palmer and Woolfe, 1999; Lapworth et al., 2001) give a much stronger account of the place of the humanistic psychotherapies within psychotherapy integration, and both texts include a focus on the development of a 'personal integration' by the psychotherapist. This is an interesting concept, which acknowledges the theoretical and clinical sophistication of the psychotherapist, as well as the uniqueness of the human relationship that lies at the core of psychotherapeutic practice. It implies greater diversification of practice, and presents interesting challenges to the researcher.

Despite the development of integrative psychotherapy, the field continues to be characterised by theoretical and methodological distinctions, and psychotherapy as a profession in the UK is structured to highlight difference rather than similarity. However, this is changing. Recent trends in Britain, such as the exercise of developing criteria for National Vocational Qualifications in Psychotherapy, have begun to highlight the common ground across modalities, and there is increasing dialogue between different psychotherapeutic 'schools'. Indeed the series of books Core Concepts in Therapy (Open University Press) aims to explore the meaning of key elements of psychotherapeutic theory across explicitly distinct psychotherapeutic models – *The Therapist's Use of Self* (Rowan and Jacobs, 2002), for example, draws on a wide range of humanistic and psychodynamic perspectives to develop a rich account of its subject.

As the psychotherapy profession in the UK moves towards statutory regulation, the felt need to retain, value and protect what is distinctive in each approach is being challenged by the imperative of professional unity in order to secure the future of psychotherapy as a valid and accountable healing force.

2

PSYCHOTHERAPY APPLICATIONS

ROBIN HOBBES

Sigmund Freud strode across the modernist world as a colossus and no discussion of psychotherapeutic application can ignore his contribution. Freud truly was the founding father of 'talking therapy', which came to be known as psychotherapy. For a time there was just this one approach – a psychoanalytically driven way of working with people. It was against this Freudian model that approaches could be evaluated as 'good' or 'bad' – the closer to Freud's original dictums, the closer the psychotherapy was to 'goodness'.

The modernist security in one truth, one approach and one understanding no longer holds in a postmodernist world. There are multiple truths, each one forming its own coherent picture of the world. The old form of objectivism in which a world could be conceived as something outside of us that we can observe and categorise is over. Instead we conceive of the world as a place of multiple truths in which coherence matters. The ability of theories to make meaning of the world, to be able to frame a part of the world into a coherent narrative is much more attractive to many of us now.

Psychotherapy is a wonderful embodiment of this postmodernist sensibility. The United Kingdom Council for Psychotherapy lists over 70 member organisations, at least 50 of whom claim some uniqueness in approach. Approaches differ from anything between a few sessions to a number of years of intensive contact between client and practitioner. It is practised in psychiatric hospitals, in doctors' surgeries, in sports institutions, in industrial organisations, in schools, in churches, in little offices in small towns and a myriad of other locations.

At times this is a difficult and confusing situation for clients and practitioners. A modernist approach would answer questions such as what type of psychotherapy is best and for what conditions does it work? A postmodernist approach can't really answer this type of question. People choose a type of psychotherapy for a variety of reasons, empirical effectiveness being only one of them. More pertinent for most people is does this type of psychotherapy fit my cultural background ... does the narrative flow of the therapy fit my values? For example psychodynamic psychotherapy tends towards a pessimistic view of the human condition whereas a humanistic and integrative approach is essentially optimistic.

The writing of this chapter has itself produced problems. How can such a large number of diverse and creative psychotherapy practices be reduced to manageable proportions? How can the reader get an idea of the wide variety of applications there are within psychotherapy? I have, primarily for reasons of economy and space, to divide this world of multiple styles, theories and methodologies into four sections: Psychodynamic, Cognitive and Behavioural, Family and Humanistic including Integrative psychotherapies. This inevitably misses out some other important approaches but hopefully other approaches can be fitted into this framework. It is hoped that the reader will take from this simplification of a fascinating complex world some route themselves that reflects their own philosophy, culture and values: then they will embark on their own unique journey through this new, wonderfully creative, professional world of psychotherapy.

Psychodynamic psychotherapy

A psychodynamic approach has its roots in the work of the early psychoanalysts including, of course, Sigmund Freud. This tradition and long history means that there is enormous diversity in the application of a psychodynamic approach. For example practitioners will vary in their emphasis on the unconscious, on dreams as a means of understanding unconscious processes or on their attention to the evolving therapeutic relationship. Some practitioners will purely focus on the 'here and now' therapeutic relationship while others will make the presence of the past in the therapeutic relationship their primary focus.

Key concepts

A psychodynamic approach holds to a number of key principles. A central tenet is the universal existence of conflict and how people manage that conflict. Inner conflicts between thoughts, feelings, desires, ideas and so on are emphasised. A young child will want the security-invoking presence of their mother but at the same time will want to be rid of her when she prevents that child from having an experience they want. A young child has intensely destructive feelings towards his mother when she denies him a chocolate bar when he is hungry. The child tries to manage what he is driven to do, think or feel (eat and enjoy the chocolate bar) and what he wishes to do, think or feel (maintain his mother's love and affection). From time to time these are in conflict with each other and with society as a whole. Mental aliveness is a continual adaptation to these conflicting forces as the individual compromises desire with social and familial appropriateness.

In order to contain intolerable states of anxiety, which arise through the experience of internal conflict, we develop a system of defences. These defences have the function of protecting us from the anxiety that arises through experiencing these unacceptable wishes.

A psychodynamic approach proposes a basic structure of the mind within which the management of these conflicts occur. This structure was described by Freud as the ego, id and superego. Essentially the id contains unconscious material and the ego and superego contain conscious and preconscious material. A key concept here is the idea of the unconscious – processes that influence us outside of awareness. A principle arising from this concept is the movement of unconscious material into consciousness or awareness leading to greater freedom and authenticity (see Chapter 1).

Past relationships, particularly with early caregivers, are considered to be of primary importance in understanding and helping the client develop healthily. These early relationships are viewed as a template or prism through which we view the world. We construct meaning and develop relationship patterns based on these early relationships. If our caregiver withheld interest in us whenever we were strongly upset we are likely to experience 'upsetness' as undesirable or wrong and prevent ourselves from this type of experience. We develop a pattern of closing down whenever we feel upset.

These early patterned styles of relationships are identified as transferential relationships by the psychotherapist. The early pattern is utilised by the client in the present when the other is perceived by the client as similar to the early caretaker. So as the client starts to feel upset in psychotherapy they shut down on this upset feeling and instead are experienced by the therapist as closing down. This is a very important concept in psychodynamic therapy as the therapeutic relationship itself and the patterns contained within it are understood as giving the client direct insight into their past experiences and how they are influencing them now.

Therapeutic application

CLIENT GROUP   A psychodynamic approach has application in individual, couple and group psychotherapy. A session will last 50 minutes and the frequency of sessions varies from weekly to as much as five times a week. Malan (1979) identified a number of key characteristics in clients for this approach to be successful. These can be divided into two areas: features of the client's lifestyle and capacities the client demonstrates in the therapeutic relationship.

In terms of lifestyle the client needs to have at least one important sustained personal relationship and be able to show the capacity to hold back from impulsive behaviour such as suicidal acts or violent acts towards self or others. The conflicts the client experiences need to be at a neurotic level – that is, not all-pervasive in the client's reactions to the world. The client needs to actively engage themselves in the therapeutic process by staying focused on one theme. The client must be motivated to engage in their own development with the therapist and be able to withstand the pressures of interpretation and confrontation that the therapist uses in their work.

Case study

Simon referred himself to a psychodynamic therapist after his second marriage failed. He talked of a marriage with little passion. He described his wife as 'very demanding' and how he would always try to accommodate her wishes, often to his own detriment. Eventually she started an affair with a mutual friend and left to set up home with him. Simon's previous marriage ended in a similar way. He had identified a pattern he was engaged in and was determined to change this pattern.

The therapist wanted to facilitate the client in realising how his past shapes his present and how his unconscious processes are influencing his conscious processes. She (the therapist) explored with Simon his early relationships in particular with his father and mother. Simon talked of a distant father who was often away from home working and an over-involved mother who turned to Simon for solace at times of loneliness. Early on in therapy Simon described his mother as all good and his father as all bad: 'She was always there for me whereas he was just a nobody'. The therapist wondered if Simon was repressing the angry, frustrating feelings he experienced with his mother and deflecting them onto his absent father.

As the therapist developed an understanding of Simon she wanted to both confront and interpret his actions, thoughts and feelings. As Simon talked about his mother she noticed a contradiction. He told a story of a mother sacrificing herself for the good of her son while at the same time this sacrificial behaviour had a strong controlling and possessive quality to it. 'She would always be there for me ... whenever I came home at night she was there waiting for me to get in. I felt I had

(Continued)

(Continued)

to be home early for her.' The therapist started to both confront and interpret what Simon revealed. 'You seem to be both loved and controlled by her'.

The therapist extended this confrontation and interpretation into the therapeutic relationship itself. She wanted to understand how past relationship patterns are being imposed by Simon on the therapeutic relationship (transference). She noticed how Simon related to her with the same expectations as he had towards his mother. He may overly accommodate what he perceives as the wishes of the therapist over his own wishes. Often on starting a therapy session Simon is preoccupied with what he thinks the therapist wants to hear from him. He always prefaced his opening remarks with 'Is that OK?'. The therapist made a confrontation of Simon's manner: 'I wonder if you will do what I want even though it may not be what you really want?'

Also she sought to understand how Simon was preventing awareness of experience by utilising defences to prevent that awareness. The therapist unexpectedly missed a planned appointment because of minor car trouble. At the next session Simon talked a lot about how angry the therapist must be with the car manufacturer. In fact he was feeling angry with the therapist for missing the appointment but repressed that feeling and displaced it onto the therapist. She wondered out loud to Simon if he was preventing himself from knowing about the angry feelings he had towards the therapist. Is this because he feared she will terminate his therapy if he is perceived as uncooperative? Simon experienced this type of intervention as allowing him to experience 'forbidden' feelings.

Simon started to develop awareness of how his past maternal relationship had influenced him. This development of awareness increased his personal freedom. He started to be able to be different with women, to relate in a more purposeful way, finding a way to relate to women that reflected a meeting of two equals.

To enable awareness to happen the psychodynamic therapist may use certain techniques or approaches. The client may be encouraged to 'freely associate' – that is, to allow anything that comes to their mind to be expressed without censorship. The therapist then listens to this 'stream of consciousness', making interpretations where appropriate. The therapist may be particularly interested in dreams the client has as this is considered the most effective way to gain access to unconscious material. Simon talked of dreams fused with anxiety in which he ran from something, he didn't know what it was. He stopped running when he hit a wall. The therapist enquired about this dream fragment. She realised that Simon's unconscious was trying to communicate something here and that Simon's task was to discover what that was. They explored together what 'running', 'walls', 'hitting' might mean. Simon recalled a memory of trying to hide from his mother when very young, of seeing a wall and wishing he could climb over it to freedom. Again Simon was processing his early experiences of being mothered.

Relationship style

Psychodynamic therapeutic relationship is very much influenced by Freud. He thought it was very important that the therapist avoid criticism, encouragement, reassurance and advice giving. Hence the relationship does not have the normal dynamics of a conventional relationship. This unusual way of being with another influences the therapeutic relationship such that often the relationship is experienced as rather cold and uninviting. This often changes as the therapeutic benefits of the work start to be experienced by the client. The therapist will not try to establish a friendship. While there will not be an absence of basic warmth, friendliness is not a priority. The therapist will primarily look to interpret and confront the actions of the patient.

Because the psychodynamic model places a lot of importance on conflict and attempts to resolve it, the therapist is interested in how conflict develops within the therapeutic relationship and will not shy away from conflictual experiences. Actually, the therapist may pay a lot of attention to attempts by the client to control the therapeutic relationship. Indeed Cooper goes so far as to say 'in successful therapy the therapist maintains control of the kind of relationship that will operate' (Cooper, 2002).

Humanistic and integrative psychotherapy

Humanistic and integrative psychotherapy embraces many different schools of psychotherapy in which there is not one accepted theoretical approach. There are, to date, 22 different organisational members within the Humanistic and Integrative section of the United Kingdom Council for Psychotherapy. Most of these 22 claim a unique theoretical and methodological approach to psychotherapy. So to condense this great variety into a few paragraphs is problematic. We can say that a humanistic approach emphasises self-actualisation with the therapist facilitating that actualisation (Rowan, 2001).

Key concepts

The world of humanistic and integrative psychotherapy is conceptually highly diverse. It will be more useful here to look at some of the general principles that can be found to lie in all schools. This approach emphasises the idea of psychotherapy as being intrinsically involved in facilitating the client's development of their potential. This potential is realised paradoxically. Essentially change involves the acceptance of who one is (and therefore 'no change') and yet also full acceptance of oneself may involve personal change. In other words someone *accepting* that they feel bad about themselves results in them developing the capacity to change and to feel good about themselves. The concepts and practices within humanistic and integrative therapy grapple with these seemingly irreconcilable dimensions of human experience.

This approach has an essentially optimistic view of human potential. People are regarded fundamentally as OK, all problems and difficulties are regarded as potentially solvable and everyone has the capacity to improve the quality of their life. Emotional problems are regarded as attempts to get on with life and as such need to be respected and understood within this framework. Only then will people be able to more effectively live their lives.

People are conceived as whole persons. So conceptually these various approaches take a wide view of people. From a humanistic perspective people are feeling, thinking and acting entities with equal importance attached to all three processes. Also spiritual dimensions of human experience are incorporated into this conceptualisation of people. From the cradle to the grave people are engaged in making meaning of their experience and using this meaning to realise their potential.

A recent very important development in humanistic psychotherapy is the emergence of integrative psychotherapy (see Chapter 1). Safran and Messer (1997) have identified three popular forms that psychotherapy integration has taken. First, there is a 'technical eclecticism' approach in which the practitioner seeks 'to determine the core ingredients different therapies might share in common, with the eventual goal of developing more efficacious treatment based on these components' (Norcross and Grencavage, 1990: 8). This is a technique-based form of integration in which the practitioner seeks to utilise in her work a variety of approaches. Reconcilable and irreconcilable theories are brought together and the practitioner selects techniques and approaches that are effective in treatment. Secondly, Safran and Messer identify a 'common principles' approach in which common factors identified in a variety of psychotherapeutic approaches are brought together. For example Nuttall (2002) argues that one such 'common principle' is the primacy of the therapeutic relationship as a factor for change. Therefore an integrative practitioner utilising this approach will pay particular attention to developing the therapeutic relationship. The last form of psychotherapy integration identified by Safran and Messer is 'theoretical integration'. The practitioner utilising this approach seeks to construct their own theory of psychotherapy that draws on other approaches. Here the practitioner seeks to devise a general unified theory of psychotherapy.

Common to most integrative practitioners is a focus on integration itself. Integration is described as 'the act of combining or adding parts to make a unified whole' (Collins, 1999). The practitioner emphasises this unifying principle in which the client is understood to be embarking on an integrative, or 'making whole', process which the therapist facilitates.

Therapeutic application

CLIENT GROUP   Humanistic and integrative psychotherapy is practised in group, couple and individual settings. Initially found exclusively in the private sector it is starting to establish itself in the public sector as more and more clients request a humanistic style of psychotherapy. Practitioners tend to work with reasonably functional clients who have a problem with a particular area of life such as relationships or work. It is, though, being found to have effectiveness with more deep-rooted problems such as personality disorder (Johnson, 2000; Bulmer, 2003; Shah, 2004). Frequency varies from a number of times a week to fortnightly or even monthly. The therapy itself can also be applied briefly or for long periods of time.

Case study

Jason referred himself to an integrative psychotherapist following a period of depression. He wanted to take a different approach to his depression from the medication his GP offered him.

An integrative practitioner pays great attention to the establishment of a working alliance. As the psychotherapy is essentially viewed as a collaborative venture in which the client is in the driving seat, the development of a bond between practitioner and client is considered as an essential ingredient for this type of psychotherapy to be effective.

Jason hoped that the therapist would 'cure' him of his depression. He acted passively, waiting for the therapist to 'do something'. The therapist was very conscious of the need to tolerate Jason's expectations of the therapy while also wanting to educate Jason into the world of psychotherapy where it is the responsibility of the client to initiate his own growth and development. The therapist spent time making an assessment with Jason. This served two functions: first she developed

(Continued)

(Continued)

a greater understanding of Jason and secondly she wove into the assessment explanations on the nature of integrative psychotherapy.

As a bond was established between Jason and the therapist, the therapy started to focus on Jason's development of self-awareness. The therapist enquired about Jason's experiences of life. This enquiry resulted in Jason enhancing his understanding of how early experiences had shaped his life. In particular he talked of having a depressed and suicidal mother and feeling responsible for keeping her alive. The therapist enquired about the sacrifices Jason felt compelled to make as a child. At first he denied making any: 'I just looked after her, my dad was working a lot. It was OK'. The therapist challenged the absence of awareness that he had to sacrifice a happy-go-lucky childhood by enquiring about what it was like to care and not play. Jason developed awareness of how he established similar patterns of caring with people in his life now. He noticed how he was attracted to people who need him to look after them.

The therapist was particularly interested in the use the client made of his growing awareness. Either Jason utilised his growing awareness towards self-actualisation or he used the awareness as a reason to not develop. Initially Jason talked of feeling, as he learnt more about himself, more depressed and being more passive. He talked of feeling strongly that the trouble in his life was 'all his own fault'. The therapist wove into the therapy the interpretation that Jason had taken decisions about his life. She emphasised that these decisions shaped and influenced the development of his life. Jason started to realise just how this had happened. The therapist alerted Jason to his ability and capacity to change these decisions. Jason's depressive mood started to lift and he developed a sense of optimism. He used his growing self-awareness to further his development.

Once the client had developed awareness then he might work through early experiences which are unresolved. The sense of wholeness that humanistic and integrative practitioners regard as central to their practice was experienced by the client as he relived past experiences with an intensity that he had denied himself originally. Jason allowed himself to feel the anger and sadness of deciding to 'give up' his childhood for his depressed mother. The therapist encouraged Jason to replay scenes from his childhood to encourage this directness of experience. For example Jason remembered coming home from school, feeling happy, to find his mother lying on the bed having taken an overdose. In the therapy room he talked to his mother as if she was actually there about what he really felt about finding her in this state. He expressed many feelings he didn't allow himself to express back then. He developed a sense of wholeness and completion around this early experience.

Finally Jason made a new commitment to live life in a way that is more commensurate with his aspirations. This is what Maslow called self-actualisation. Jason took career and relationship decisions that resulted in a greater sense of achievement and well-being.

Relationship style

The humanistic and integrative practitioner pays a lot of attention to the therapeutic relationship. This is seen as central to the psychotherapy. The relationship is conceived as the space in which becoming whole or integration occurs. The therapist will seek to develop an authentic relationship in which Rogers' core conditions of empathy, congruence and respect flourish.

The therapeutic relationship is developed through dialogue. There is an emphasis on what Clarkson calls the 'I–You relationship' (Clarkson, 1992) – that is, what is occurring in the present between therapist and client. The practitioner does not seek to be anything more than he or she is at that time. They will not hide behind theory or methodology. The practitioner seeks to be flexible, responsive and involved with their clients. Early on in the therapy with Jason the therapist found Jason's passivity and lack of involvement in the therapy challenging. Initially adopting an accepting stance to this the therapist started to question whether their approach was being effective. She decided to be more present and talk about the frustration and despair in her experience when being with Jason. This moved the therapeutic relationship on to a more 'real' basis. By the end of the psychotherapy we have two people who are autonomous and mutually respectful of the differences and similarities between them. By the time Jason left therapy he had experienced the therapist as a person like him who has strengths and weaknesses. He experienced the psychotherapy as a two-person encounter in which both people's experience is included (Stark, 2000).

Cognitive behavioural therapy (CBT)

Cognitive and behavioural therapy (CBT) is a collective description of a number of approaches. Central to this approach is the idea that identifying and changing unhelpful thoughts and behaviours results in the development of psychological well-being.

Key concepts

CBT's scientific, experimental background has and continues to have a major influence on the key concepts held. The key concepts are based on observation. Behaviour and thinking are given primary importance and, unlike many other psychotherapies, there is little conceptualisation of emotional states. The CBT therapist is not particularly interested *per se* in what the client is feeling. She is interested in what the client is thinking and doing. Classical conditioning, in which the capacity to associate a new stimuli with the effects of that stimuli (the ringing bell as mentioned in Chapter 1) and operant conditioning, contribute to the conceptual foundation. Operant conditioning conceptualises the process of change and development. The concept allows for an understanding of how people develop and claims that the consequences of behaviour have a primary influence on the behaviour being repeated. For example we will keep on doing something if we receive a positive response to what it is we do; a smile for doing something for someone results in the doer doing this more. It is now possible to develop ways to influence people through reinforcing 'good' behaviours and ignoring 'bad' ones.

The problem with the idea that positive reinforcement results in increased behaviour is that there are many examples of people doing things where the results are not particularly pleasurable. To explain this behaviourists developed the idea of habituation. We repeat behaviour when we experience some sort of gain from it. If an overly anxious person experiences a sense of security through realising their front door is locked they might start to double-check that their front door is locked to encourage a sense of security.

The behaviourists needed to incorporate the world of both thoughts and emotions into their conceptualisation for the theory to effectively explain dysfunctional emotional states. Beck's concept of schemata – cognitive structures in the mind that filter and organise incoming data – provided just the bridge behaviourists were looking for (see Chapter 1).

Therapeutic application

CLIENT GROUP CBT is primarily used in a one-to-one setting. The psychotherapy is symptom-based. It is practised with a wide client group demonstrating effectiveness with anxiety and mood disorders, personality disorders and psychotic states (National Institute for Clinical Excellence, 2005). The client needs to be motivated to work on themselves and to focus purposefully on symptom removal. The client and therapist define clearly the outcome desired from the therapy and thus measure its success in terms of symptom removal. A key ingredient in the effectiveness of CBT is the clients' willingness to engage in activities between sessions. This is called homework and clients will be set homework between sessions and discuss the application of the homework when in sessions.

Case study

Maria was referred by her GP for CBT following severe panic attacks when taking a holiday flight. Maria agreed with her therapist to meet for eight sessions in which she would approach the development of secure feelings when flying in a systematic and structured way.

First of all the therapist made a detailed assessment of what Maria did when she was about to fly in an aeroplane. The therapist was interested in all that Maria does when both flying and in preparation for the flight. The therapist also wanted to know what Maria was thinking before flying and while flying. From this information a detailed construction was made concerning the symptom. Hypotheses were discussed and arrived at as to how Maria might be contributing to the anxiety in both what she does and what she thinks when on an aeroplane.

The therapist decided to use two approaches. First she decided to encourage Maria to engage in a structured exposure to the feared situation. Maria was to gradually expose herself to aeroplanes starting with observing them at airports, visiting stationary aeroplanes, building up to eventually flying again. Maria undertook homework in which she engaged in this plan of exposure. At the same time the therapist encouraged Maria to identify an ally who would accompany her on these assignments to support her changing her response to flying. Gradually Maria built up a new habituation to flying which included the experience of security.

Secondly the therapist used a cognitive approach. Maria was encouraged to share the thoughts she had about flying being a dangerous activity. The therapist confronted Maria's thinking that flying is dangerous with the facts on the safety of flying. Maria was encouraged to do some research into the safety record of aeroplanes as a mode of transport. Maria was asked to involve her ally in correcting any faulty thinking she displayed while desensitising herself to aeroplanes. The ally was also encouraged to help Maria to think accurately about flying and its actual risks. Taking this approach Maria was able to develop the capacity to experience security when taking a flight.

Relationship style

The therapeutic relationship is primarily task-oriented. Maria and her therapist demonstrated the ability to identify and work on tasks. This has a major influence on the therapeutic relationship. The role of the therapist was to provide information and to influence the session so that it takes an appropriate direction related to Maria's goals. At the same time Maria needed to be purposeful and engaged in the therapy, and willing to invest time and energy between sessions.

The importance of the therapist as a person is much less with this type of therapy. The therapist does not disclose aspects of their own experience in being with the client. Therapists are advised to not use interpretation and excessive reassurance. Similarly enquiring into the full nature of the client's experience is cautioned against as is an evaluative therapeutic response. Maria's therapist confined her enquiry solely to Maria's experience of flight. Interestingly there has been considerable interest amongst CBT practitioners over the effectiveness of this type of therapy when there is the absence of a therapist during the delivery of the therapy. Therapeutic programmes using computers, books and telephone contact have been evaluated and show some effectiveness.

It must be added that there is great diversity in the CBT world and its wide application means any description of an approach will not do justice to this diversity. For example there have been very interesting developments in the field in relation to the development of the therapeutic relationship within CBT treatment (Wills and Sanders, 1997; Dryden, 2001).

Family therapy

It was in the 1950s that family therapy started to establish itself as a separate and distinct school of psychotherapy. In this approach the family unit becomes the focus for the therapist and, importantly, the therapist works with as many family members as possible. No longer does the therapist see an individual in her office; rather she insists on seeing the whole family – there are no individual problems, only family problems. In many ways the therapist becomes a group worker.

Key concepts

From a family therapy perspective psychological problems are developed within the family. The family also sustains and nurtures these problems. To understand these problems the therapist needs to understand the interactional patterns surrounding the problem. How does the family relate to each other when the problem occurs and when they are reflecting on the problem?

The family is conceived as a system. This means that members of a family all influence and affect each other. This influence may be direct or indirect. A system seeks to maintain a level of harmony and balance called homeostasis. Actions within the system can be considered in terms of succeeding or not succeeding in the maintenance of homeostasis. The way a family attempts to solve its problems is understood as the unique way that particular family maintains its status quo or homeostasis.

Every system has boundaries and these boundaries themselves vary in their permeability. For example some families are very insular and have little contact with the outside world – here we would say the boundaries are impermeable – whereas other families have highly permeable boundaries in which other systems such as police or social work agencies are actively involved with the family – permeable boundaries.

Within the family system there will be designated roles. These are actions and activities that are assigned to various family members. These roles may be obvious and clearly enforced but also they may be much more subtly implied and enforced. A child may be designated a 'trouble maker'. The family always refers to this member as 'always in trouble' and subtly reinforces this role by smiling and inadvertently encouraging the 'trouble maker'. A complex system of rules will operate within the family designed to maintain the system the family has created through maintenance of roles within that system. There will be hierarchies and structures that help to sustain the roles and rules within the family. The mother is always the 'caregiver', the son the 'rebel' and the father the 'punisher', for example.

Family therapists distinguish between process and content. The process will be the activities used by the family members to maintain the family system. The family therapist conceptualises communication patterns in terms of how something is said rather than in terms of what is said. The non-verbal components of expression give clues as to the way the family system maintains itself. Any change to the family system that will sustain itself needs to be effective on the process level rather than the content level. In other words therapeutic interventions must affect the way the family communicates. For example the result of an effective intervention will be family members not smiling when they are expressing disapproval of each other. Interventions are designed to affect the way family members respond to each other rather than affect the content of the communication between family members.

Therapeutic application

CLIENT GROUP Family therapy is mostly practised within the public sector and is found in social services departments and the NHS. There is a small amount of private practice within the UK. Most families are referred by other professionals for family therapy. The client group is the family. Ideally the therapist will want to see all members of the family that are actively involved in that family system. Family therapy is not a long-term therapy and will not normally last more than a few months. The frequency also is variable ranging from weekly to monthly.

Case study

The Thompson family are referred for family therapy. Gill, a 15-year-old, is getting into trouble with the police and school. Gill has a younger 13-year-old brother called Sammy. She lives with her mother and stepfather.

The therapist worked within a team of family therapists. Their purpose-built office had a room in which there was a two-way mirror behind which a team of therapists observed the therapist working with the family. The therapist used the observing team as consultants to aid in the development of intervention strategies that will influence the family system. The family was aware that a team of observers were behind the two-way mirror but the observing therapeutic team do not have any direct contact with the family.

On meeting the family the therapist wished to discover this family system, the roles within it and the style of communication the family used. This was done in a variety of ways. First the therapist asked about the presenting problem. As the family talked about the trouble Gill was getting into they started to show the conflicts and challenges the family had reported. A great deal of shouting, gesticulating and general protesting behaviour happened in the therapy room. Gill was often related to and described as 'always being difficult', whereas her brother was seen as 'no trouble at all'. At the same time Gill would act as a trouble maker in the room while Sammy kept quiet.

The therapist decided to construct a genogram, which is in essence a family tree. The genogram enabled the family to identify its various members. As the family talked about its past and current members, information started to emerge of this family's specific hierarchy and 'influencing members'. This helped the therapists to draw up a family history. It emerged that Gill's father died a number of years ago and the mother had remarried recently.

The therapist started to gather information on the family's boundaries and roles. The observing team noticed that whenever Gill started to talk about herself, her mother interrupted and brought herself into the picture. They concluded that there were highly impermeable boundaries between Gill and her mother. The team also noticed how any expression of emotion by Gill or her brother over the loss of their father created disturbance in the mother. She agitated and again interrupted other people's conversations.

(Continued)

The family met with the therapist for a number of weeks and started to establish a good working relationship. The team recommended to the therapist that he use a technique to facilitate the family to talk about what they found particularly difficult to discuss. The therapist used a technique called a 'family sculpt'. Here a member of the family, in this case Gill's brother, was asked to create a living tableau with the family that represented their understanding of the family system. In this tableau Gill was placed standing on a chair towering over the rest of the family, who in turn were placed in various uncomfortable positions around her. The therapist asked Sammy to bring in his real father and place him somewhere in the room. Nervously he put the dead father, represented by a cushion, on the top of Gill's head. This acted as a permission to the family to start to talk about the impact the loss of the father had on them all.

The observing team of therapists noticed how the stepfather remained a shadowy figure within the family. They decided to recommend to the therapist in the room an intervention to encourage the stepfather to participate more actively in the family. The therapist directly invited the stepfather to participate in the sessions by asking him about his responses to what another member of the family had said. This failed. The rest of the family became highly conflictual, arguing and loudly diverting themselves from his presence. The team decided to advise the therapist to use a reframing intervention. The therapist described the family as not ready to have the stepfather involved in their lives and recommended that they do what they can to prevent him getting involved. Over time this had the intention the team hoped for, with the family 'resisting' the therapists' advice and allowing a much more active involvement from the stepfather.

Towards the end of the therapy the family system has started to change. The family created stronger boundaries between the mother and Gill. The stepfather started to develop and sustain a more active role within the family. They started to accept his presence as an active member within the system. This had the effect of Gill conforming more effectively to the pressures of authority and getting better grades at school.

Relationship style

Family therapists are not particularly interested in the development of a therapeutic relationship. They use the term 'therapy role' rather than relationship. The therapist maintains a complex role relationship throughout the therapy. They need to stay outside of the system maintaining the neutrality of an observer. At the same time the therapist seeks to establish involvement and activity within the system so as to effectively influence it. This seemingly contradictory approach provides stimulating challenges for the therapist. When do they stay outside of the system and when do they make an intervention? The use of an observing team of therapists greatly helps resolve this dilemma. Finally, the therapist does not share their experience with the family. Indeed the therapeutic relationship is more akin to that developed by cognitive and behavioural therapists.

3

THE EVIDENCE BASE OF PSYCHOTHERAPY

MELANIE EPSTEIN

The need for psychotherapists to work within the context of evidence-based practice is becoming a vital part of ethical and professional practice. There has been a growing movement stemming from political, social and economic forces towards collecting and disseminating research results indicating which therapies have been shown to 'work'. The choice of evidence has profound effects on the way research is interpreted, the directions of future research and on the future direction of psychotherapy practice. There are current trends both to create a scientific paradigm of standardised research criteria and methodologies, as well as attempts to create an integrative or pan-theoretical framework of common factors. In what the uninitiated might think of as the dry world of psychotherapy research, there is a great deal of emotion on both sides of the debate. This chapter will explore the evidence base of psychotherapy in connection with this debate. The focus will be on individual therapy, and the evidence base for the humanistic therapies.

In the same way as an understanding of a client's history, social and cultural context is necessary to understand their presentation, build the therapeutic relationship and facilitate their personal journey, so an understanding of the roots of psychotherapy research is important to illuminate the current field. This section of the chapter will review some of the major questions that have been asked in psychotherapy research and the conclusions and narrative that have been derived from these questions.

Further information about the history of, and phases in, psychotherapy research can be found in the comprehensive chapters written by Barkham (2002) and Orlinsky and Russell (1994).

What is psychotherapy?

The phase of discovery (pre-1950)
Many texts focus on psychotherapy research after the 1950s. That is the time when psychotherapy research evolved in the United

Kingdom. However the roots of most current trends existing within psychotherapy research can be seen during the pioneering days of the development of psychotherapy.

Freud's development of psychoanalysis incorporated his cultural milieu in turn-of-the-century Vienna as well as the traditions of the parent field of clinical medicine and neurology. This included the argument over how much is 'art' and how much is 'science'. Freud was one of the first writers to comment explicitly on the importance and impact of the relationship between therapist and client (Freud, 1912/1958, 1913/1966). He identified three aspects of the therapeutic relationship: transference, countertransference and the client's friendly and positive linking of the therapist with benevolent and kind personas from the past. This last aspect is what has been reformulated and developed into the concept of the *therapeutic or working alliance*. Freud was asked to prove that his 'talking cure' worked. He dismissed his critics with the claim that his case study method would prove his point. Anyone who had been properly trained in the practice of psychoanalysis would obtain results comparable to his own. He was also sceptical about 'statistics' as he believed that clinical information available was too diverse and heterogeneous to compare. These arguments have continued to pervade the world of psychotherapy research.

Freud's work raised the broad question 'Does psychotherapy work?' Despite Freud's views on research, treatment centres associated with psychoanalytic training institutes began to collect systematic data on treatment results. The first statistical tabulations were published in the late 1920s by authors such as Fenichel, Huddleson and Matz (cited in Orlinsky and Russell, 1994).

A further development of Freud's method of case study research can be seen in the work of Henry Murray and his colleagues who worked in the field of personality research. He combined elements of the psychoanalytic case study with the scientific methods of his day. His 'multiform method' involved using different sources of information, as well as different interpretations of the information (Murray, 1938). We see here the roots of *pluralist* methodology where quantitative as well as qualitative methods are used (Howard, 1983).

The roots of psychotherapy process research go back particularly to Carl Rogers and his use of phonographic recordings of counselling sessions in the early 1940s. He inspired a generation of researchers and together with his co-workers at the University of Chicago Counseling Center organised one of the first major long-term programmes of process and outcome research in the field

(Gordon et al., 1954). Rogers managed to combine the latest scientific technology with a clinician's view of the importance of the clinical relevance of his research. He also provided the basis for the research into the therapeutic alliance, with his description of the necessary and sufficient conditions for therapeutic change (Rogers, 1957). He claimed that a relationship with a therapist who would provide the facilitative conditions of congruence, unconditional positive regard and empathic understanding would activate the innate healing and growth potential in the client. Rogers also had an important impact on rating psychotherapy process with his development of scales such as the Experiencing Scale for measuring the depth of client exploration, and a nine-point scale for measuring empathy. These rating scales were later developed and widely used for training therapists as well as for further research.

Does psychotherapy work?

The 'no' answer

The phase of verification in psychotherapy research was launched internationally by the British psychologist Hans Eysenck (1952). In his landmark review of 24 studies of psychotherapy outcome, he claimed that there was no research evidence to support the effectiveness of psychotherapy, and that psychoanalysis was less effective than no therapy at all. He drew on existing data to determine information about the rate of spontaneous improvement in neurotic people who received no formal psychotherapeutic treatment. He purported to show that the 'spontaneous remission rate' in the untreated patients was about two-thirds, which was identical if not higher than the improvement rate for treated cases quoted by Fenichel and others in 19 published reports on psychotherapy outcome at that time. It is ironic that his work provided such an enormous impetus to subsequent research, and also that his data actually supported the efficacy of psychotherapy. Eysenck later recanted on his anti-therapy stance. His work has subsequently been re-evaluated and critiqued by for example Bergin and Lambert (1978), who re-analysed Eysenck's coding and showed that a range of different conclusions could have been reached on the basis of different codings of the original data. Bergin and Lambert (1978) found the rate for spontaneous remission to be 43 per cent rather than 67 per cent. Eysenck was a behaviourist who was highly critical of therapy research generated outside the behavioural framework. In more recent times, Luborsky et al. (1999), among others, have written about how researcher allegiance exerts a powerful effect on the research literature and needs to be overtly taken into account.

Eysenck's work provided an enormous impetus to subsequent research. This demonstrates the importance of repeating research to ensure that the results are as they seem. This is particularly true in today's context of evidence-based practice. Many clinicians sensed that Eysenck's conclusions were at odds with their clinical experience and took up the challenge of whether psychotherapy did indeed work. Eysenck's work stimulated research that would answer his question from the same frame of reference and with similar methodology as his. He provided the catalyst whereby psychotherapy research became 'science', not 'art'. At that point in time, psychotherapy research incorporated a scientific method or positivist methodology. Qualitative methods, and some of the multiple sources of information as well as the uniqueness of individual clients, as in Murray's multiform method (1938), became split off and marginalised from mainstream psychotherapy research.

Controlled studies

One of the results of Eysenck's work was to stimulate the inclusion of comparison groups in psychotherapy outcome studies. This meant that patients were assigned to a treatment group or waiting-list or no-treatment control group, thus allowing for a comparison of treated with untreated clients. Attempts were made to make the groups equivalent by matching for important dimensions such as psychopathology. This is done by matching groups on categorical classifications such as the *Diagnostic and Statistical Manual of Mental Disorders* (DSM – as used predominantly in the United States) (American Psychiatric Association, 1980, 1994) and the International Classification of Diseases (ICD), as used primarily in Great Britain. The most common way to do this has been to use Axis I (clinical disorders, such as anxiety disorders or depressive disorders). Over the last 20 years, however, there has been increasing discussion regarding the relationship between personality disorders (Axis II) and Axis I disorders. The extremely high rates of concurrent Axis I disorders in people with personality disorder diagnoses (found in diverse samples assessed by different methods), as well as the high rates of Axis II disorders found in people with Axis I disorders, raises questions regarding the independence and distinctiveness of these disorders (First et al., 2002). This may lead to questions about the research that focuses on Axis I criteria without mention of Axis II.

The 'yes' answer – psychotherapy does work

Smith and Glass (1977) developed a new type of statistical analysis, namely meta-analysis, of 475 controlled outcome studies. This is a statistical procedure that enables data from separate studies to be considered collectively through the calculation of an effect size from each investigation. This was elaborated on in their book *The Benefits of Psychotherapy* (Smith et al., 1980). The development of this type of meta-analysis, as well as the nature of research included, set the scene for the further documentation of research into psychotherapy. In this meta-analysis, these authors suggest that at the end of treatment, the average psychotherapy patient is better off than 80 per cent of the untreated sample. Similarly, Lambert et al. (1986) have suggested at least a 70 per cent improvement for treated patients, and an improvement rate of about 40 per cent in untreated patients. However, they comment that the control group includes some patients who seek treatment elsewhere, whilst serving as controls in treatment studies! Other major reviews, for example Lambert and Bergin (1992), include as the first two achievements of psychotherapy research, the demonstration that the general effects of psychotherapy exceed those of spontaneous remission, and the demonstration that these therapy effects were generally positive.

Over 60 years of reviews of psychotherapy outcome research now document the evidence supporting the effectiveness of psychotherapy (Bergin, 1971; Bergin and Lambert, 1978; Elliot, 2001; Lambert and Bergin, 1992; Lambert et al., 1986; Meltzoff and Kornreich, 1970; Parry, 2000; Smith et al., 1980; Stubbs and Bozarth, 1994). These reviews include studies on thousands of clients, hundreds of therapies, a wide range of presenting problems, and diverse therapeutic approaches. A wide range of measures of change has been used. These incorporate the perspectives of therapists, clients, their families and society.

Linked with the research about the effectiveness of therapy is the information relating to the temporal course of improvement in therapy. The road to recovery is short for the majority of people receiving therapy. About two-thirds of people who do seek psychotherapy are improved in about two months (Howard et al., 1986; McNeilly and Howard, 1991). A meta-analysis by Howard and his colleagues (Howard et al., 1986), as well as a session-by-session analysis of patient progress (Kadera et al., 1996) found that about 75 per cent of clients significantly improved after 26 sessions or 6 months of weekly psychotherapy. The investigators also found that, even with as few as 8 to 10 sessions, approximately 50 per cent of clients show *clinically* significant change.

Does humanistic therapy work?

Humanistic therapies may not be included in reviews of psy-chotherapy research, or considered in criteria for evidence-based practice. There are many reasons for this. The criteria used for inclusion in reviews favour positivist or natural science research methods over human science or qualitative methods that may be used for the purposes of exploring and understanding clients' sub-jective realities. Many studies use single-group designs so are not usually included in meta-analyses. Some of the research that was not originally incorporated into the literature in the 1950s when it came out, is still overlooked. Literature that has been published in German is not included in the American literature, or in British publications such as the review by Roth and Fonagy (1996). Some of the literature uses new labels (e.g. process-experiential therapy or emotionally focused). As a result, humanistic therapies are some-times dismissed as lacking in empirical support. In order to coun-teract some of these trends, Cain and Seeman (2001) have collated the research on humanistic therapy in a handbook on humanistic research and practice.

Robert Elliot (2001: 57–81) conducted the largest meta-analysis of humanistic therapy outcome research to date. He analysed 99 therapy conditions in 86 studies involving over 5,000 clients. Studies reviewed covered client-centred therapy, 'non-directive' therapies, task-focused process-experiential therapies, emotionally focused therapy for couples, Gestalt therapy, encounter sensitivity groups and other experiential/humanistic therapies. He concluded the following:

1 Clients who participate in humanistic therapies show, on average, large amounts of change over time.
2 Post-therapy gains in humanistic therapies are stable; they are main-tained over early (<12 months) and late (12 months) follow-ups.
3 In randomised clinical trials with untreated control clients, clients who participate in humanistic therapies generally show substantially more change than comparable untreated clients.
4 In randomised clinical trials with comparative treatment control clients, clients in humanistic therapies generally show amounts of change equivalent to clients in non-humanistic therapies, including CBT (Cognitive Behavioural Therapy).

(Elliot, 2001: 71)

The results are compatible with the other findings listed that different types of psychotherapy, including humanistic psychotherapy, are effective. This summary does not address the question of where humanistic therapies may be particularly effective, or the types of questions that might be asked by humanistic therapist-researchers that would not be asked by other modalities.

What works for whom and when?

This type of research started to develop from the 1960s. This was around the time of the development of behaviour therapy, as well as of an exponential increase in the number and type of psychotherapies. It has been carried out with the view that clients will respond similarly to different interventions, different therapists and therapies as well as during the course of therapy. The tools of this type of research are the randomised controlled trial (RCT), as well as the use of treatment manuals and protocols for therapists. This may include a group who receive waiting list or no treatment, and/or a group of patients who receive placebo treatment (placebo drug or therapy). One example of this is the National Institute of Mental Health Treatment of Depression Collaborative Research Program (NIMH TDRCP: Elkin, 1994; Elkin et al., 1989). In this study, 250 clients in three different research sites were randomly assigned to one of four different groups. These groups comprised two psychotherapy treatment conditions (cognitive behaviour therapy and interpersonal therapy), and two non-psychotherapy treatment conditions. These latter were clinical management together with antidepressant medication (imipramine) or a placebo. This last group was to act as a control for the drug condition as well as for the psychotherapy group. In this design, expert therapists were used in the two differing psychotherapies, the varying treatments were documented in manuals, and the therapists' adherence to treatment protocols was verified. All four groups showed statistically significant improvement from before to after treatment, including the group who received placebo treatment. There was no evidence of any difference between the two psychotherapies in their ability to reduce depressive and general symptoms or improve functioning.

An example of this type of research in the UK is the Sheffield Psychotherapy project. A programme of research has compared prescriptive and exploratory therapy for clients with anxiety and depression under a range of conditions. (For more details of this project and other programmes of research, see the review edited by Beutler and Crago, 1991.)

The methodology for these types of studies is elaborated and critiqued in Roth and Fonagy (1996) and Bower and King (2000). McLeod (2000) has written a critique of the prevailing use of quantitative methods in studying psychotherapy outcome.

The outcome for these types of studies has been summarised by Stiles et al. (1986) with the question 'Are all psychotherapies equivalent?' They suggest three possible mechanisms for the evidence suggesting that they are indeed more or less equivalent:

1 Research methods have not been stringent enough to detect differences.
2 Different therapies may be broadly equivalent due to the overriding effects of common factors.
3 Research strategies have not been appropriate to detect existing differences.

What is the drug metaphor model?

The search for the 'active ingredients' of therapy has led to research design which uses some of the principles used in research into the therapeutic effects of drugs and pharmacologically active substances. In this paradigm, psychotherapy is viewed as comprising active ingredients (supplied by the therapist) to the client. These active ingredients are process components, which can be measured. If a component is an active ingredient, then a high level leads to a positive outcome. If it does not, the ingredient is supposed to be inert. In medical research, the use of a placebo (a pharmacologically inert substance named from the Latin 'I shall please') has long been thought to enable researchers to determine the amount of change related to the active ingredients of a drug under study, and to control for psychological factors. This has been translated into psychotherapy research. This model has been critiqued as an oversimplification of what happens in a therapy situation (e.g. Stiles and Shapiro, 1989).

Frank and Frank (1991) use the drug metaphor in a creative way to make the case for the commonalities between the different forms of therapy:

> Two such apparently different psychotherapies as psychoanalysis and systematic desensitisation could be like penicillin and digitalis – totally different pharmacologic agents suitable for totally different conditions. On the other hand, the active therapeutic ingredient of both could be the same, analogous to two aspirin-containing compounds marketed under different names. We believe the second is closer to the truth (1991: 39).

How does psychotherapy work?

Process research investigates how changes take place within and between sessions, and is linked with theories of change.

Table 3.1   *The drug metaphor model*

Assumptions of drug metaphor[1]	Critique of drug metaphor
Process and outcome are readily distinguishable from and bear a simple cause–effect relationship to one another	Possibility of outcome-process effects. Consideration of more than two levels of a process variable
Component names refer to components of consistent content and scope	Consideration of the alliance, and the stage of therapy
The potentially active ingredients are known and measured or manipulated	Influence of variables other than therapist technique and client variables upon the process–outcome relationship
The active ingredients are contained in the therapist's behaviour with the client taking a passive role	The therapist's in-session behaviour is influenced by client requirements and response. The impact of client variables, other than *DSM IV* Axis I diagnosis
There is a directly proportional response to the 'dose' of what is being measured	The possibility of non-linear relationships between process and outcome
The best way to demonstrate a psychotherapeutic procedure's efficiency is by controlled clinical trial	Each therapy situation is unique. Different therapies may need different methods and criteria for evaluation

[1]Adapted from Shapiro et al. (1994).

Rogers provided the initial impetus for this work in the United States, and prompted a great deal of research into empathy and the facilitative conditions. This later developed into research on the therapeutic alliance. In Britain, process research followed a different pattern. The key focus here was looking at the relationship between process and overall outcomes in relation to examining the specific effects of different therapeutic approaches. The methodology developed for this type of research has been predominantly quantitative. There has been associated great debate concerning the respective roles of specific and common factors in facilitating therapeutic change.

More recently, researchers have recognised that there is no long-term change without short-term change. In this way the micro-processes that occur within specific change events can be studied, rather than relating process to the overall outcome of therapy. This has led to a number of overarching models for understanding the process of change that are not linked to one type of therapy or another. Some examples of these are:

1 Elliot and Shapiro (1992) have examined significant therapy events, which are portions of therapy sessions in which clients experience a meaningful degree of change or help.

2 Intensive process analysis (Rice and Greenberg, 1984) examines the contextual meaning of significant events in therapy. This model has been used to study ruptures in the therapeutic alliance, their links to patients' characteristic patterns, and to develop and test a model of the skilful resolution of these problematic events (Parry, 2000; Safran et al., 1990).

3 The assimilation model was developed by Stiles et al. (1990). This model focuses on the stages of working through problematic or painful experiences on a continuum of eight stages from 'warded off' to 'mastery'. It can be used as a guiding assessment procedure, to direct therapists' attention to help clients move along the continuum, as well as a way of evaluating the impact of therapy. Clinical examples of the use of this derived from the Sheffield Psychotherapy Projects can be found in Barkham et al. (1996).

4 The Core Conflictual Relationship Theme Method (CCRT) identifies narrative episodes describing relationships with significant others (Luborsky et al., 1986). CCRT patterns are pervasive across relationships with different types of people, consistent across different measurement periods and reflect improvement during the course of therapy. CCRT patterns with the client and therapist during therapy are similar to descriptions of the client's relationships with others outside of treatment. CCRT research produces strong evidence in support of the Freudian concept of transference.

What are the links between process and outcome in determining change?

In a review of more than 2,000 process–outcome studies Orlinsky et al. (1994: 361) conclude the following:

1 The quality of the client's participation in therapy is the most important determinant of outcome.

2 The therapeutic bond, *especially as perceived by the patient*, is importantly involved in mediating the process–outcome link.

3 The therapist's contribution is mainly through empathic, affirmative, collaborative and self-congruent engagement with the client and the skilful application of potent interventions.

4 These consistent findings … can be considered *facts* established by 40-plus years of research on psychotherapy. (italics not present in original)

Shapiro et al. (1994: 30) conclude that 'therapist interventions are not shown by the available, conventional process–outcome analysis to exert strong effects upon the effectiveness of treatment'.

A large amount of research on the relationship between process and outcome has been designed from the viewpoint of the 'drug metaphor', that they are linear and directly proportional. This has been critiqued because of the phenomenon of *responsiveness*, the fact that participants' behaviour is affected by emerging context (Stiles et al., 1998). Therapists tend to respond to a client's emerging needs with appropriate interventions. In successful therapy, clients experience optimum levels of these interventions. Clients who need less may receive less, and their measured outcomes may be just as good as clients who needed more, and received more. Therefore process components do not predict outcome in a simple way. They may have no or negative correlation with outcome (Stiles et al., 1998). The way that this research is carried out is being reconceptualised. The current trend is to move outcome and process research in the direction of the practitioner, and to combine them into a single activity. In this way change is seen as the process of achieving small outcomes. These become in turn processes towards further outcomes. There is now increasing use of qualitative methods to look at process, and the individual is becoming prioritised in outcomes research.

What is the link between the dodo bird and the common factors?

Freud started the modern age of psychotherapy. However, it did not take long for Freud's followers to break ranks and Jung, Adler, Rank and Ferenczi all started to proclaim their theoretical differences and promoted new theories. This process of division and creation of new theories has continued with an exponential increase in forms and orientations of psychotherapy. Estimates of at least 200 therapy models, with more than 400 associated techniques, have been made (Garfield and Bergin, 1994). Garfield has predicted that 'sometime in the next century there will be one form of psychotherapy for every adult in the Western World' (1987: 98). Investigators have tried to prove empirically that 'their therapy' is the best. This has been seen with the use of the drug metaphor in the age of comparative clinical trials and the question, 'what therapy works best?'. Bergin and Lambert described the ulterior motive behind this as 'presumably, the one shown to be most effective will prove that position to be correct and will serve as a demonstration that the "losers" should be persuaded to give up their views' (1978: 162). However, this premise of these comparative studies has not been borne out (Norcross and Newman, 1992). This finding of no significant difference between therapies has been named the dodo bird verdict (Luborsky et al., 1975). Borrowed from *Alice in Wonderland*, it says, 'Everyone has won and so all must have prizes'. On a less jocular note, Hubble et al. (1999) warn of the perils for those therapists who allow themselves to be marginalised by mainstream research by saying 'unless clinicians come together, they may find themselves sharing the same status as the real dodo bird of Mauritius and Reunion – extinct' (1999: 11). The dodo bird verdict has led to the emergence of an alternative research strand, which has been to identify the common therapeutic factors or pan-theoretical elements. This has both arisen from and contributed to the field of psychotherapy integration. This is a systematic way of combining two or more elements of therapy within a coherent over-arching theoretical structure. Those interested in psychotherapy integration have suggested that common factors cut across different approaches to therapy and make them all equally effective (Arkowitz, 1992; Goldfried and Padawer, 1982).

However, the radical suggestion that the effectiveness of different forms of therapy approaches was related to their common elements was made as early as 1936 during the pre-1950s phase of discovery (Rosenzweig, 1936). In particular Rosenzweig highlighted the relationship between client and clinician as being one of the most important common factors.

Frank wrote about therapy within the wider context of methods of bringing about healing (1961, 1973; Frank and Frank, 1991). From about 1980 onwards, a large amount of writing about the common factors started to appear. Weinberger (1995: 45–69) noted that a positive relationship exists between year of publication and the number of common factor proposals offered.

Frank and Frank (1991: 40–3) identified four features shared by all effective therapies:

1 'an emotionally charged, confiding relationship with a helping person'
2 'a healing setting'
3 'a rationale, conceptual scheme or myth that provides a plausible explanation for the patient's symptoms and describes a ritual or procedure for resolving them'
4 'a ritual or procedure that requires the active participation of both patient and therapist and that is believed to be the means of restoring the patient's health'

In 1992 Lambert proposed four therapeutic factors as the principal elements accounting for client change. These were based on a broad range of research methods over decades of time. He later documented the percentage role of each factor in determining therapeutic outcome (Asay and Lambert, 1999):

1   Client/extratherapeutic factors (40 per cent)
    These are factors that are part of the client and part of the environment that help in recovery, regardless of participation in therapy.
2   Therapeutic relationship (30 per cent)
    This includes a host of variables found in a variety of therapies regardless of the therapist's orientation.
3   Technique (15 per cent)
    These are factors or interventions unique to specific therapies.
4   Hope (15 per cent)
    This refers to the client's expectation that he will be helped.

This may seem surprising given the emphasis in much of the literature on the role of the therapist and the techniques used in different models as the key factors determining therapeutic outcome.

What are the big four common therapeutic factors?

Hubble et al. (1999) have taken up the idea of the 'Big Four' in a handbook designed to provide an overview of the research, and to suggest how the common factors research might be put into practice. This is written with a view to providing a bridge between the various schools of therapy, as well as between research and clinical practice.

1 Client/extratherapeutic factors

Many written accounts of therapy emphasise the therapist's contribution, with the client seen as a passive recipient of the therapist's wisdom. However in a poll conducted by Norcross (1986), therapists attributed 67 per cent of the variance in outcome to the client. Lambert (1992) attributes 40 per cent of the outcome variance in therapy to extratherapeutic factors, which consist of the client and factors in the client's life. This is whatever clients bring to the therapy room. This includes the personal characteristics of clients, their supports and resources in their lives, including random events such as chance. The client contribution to outcome has been put as high as 70 per cent (Norcross, 1986; Tallman and Bohart, 1999). Tallman and Bohart state:

We believe the dodo bird verdict occurs because the client's abilities to use whatever is offered surpass any differences that might exist in techniques or approaches ... Clients utilize and tailor what each approach provides to address their problems. (1999: 95, italics in original)

Bergin and Garfield (1994) observe that

... it is the client more than the therapist who implements the change process ... Rather than argue over whether or not 'therapy works' we could address ourselves to the question of whether or not 'the client works'! (1994: 825).

The research on client factors in therapy is reviewed comprehensively in Bergin and Garfield (1994) and Tallman and Bohart (1999).

2   The therapeutic relationship

Researchers acknowledge, and many clinicians understand by experience, the central role of the therapist– client relationship in the process of psychotherapy and client change (Gelso and Carter, 1985; Greenberg and Pinsoff, 1986; Rogers, 1957). The quality of the therapeutic relationship has been shown to be a significant determinant of positive outcome across varying types of psychotherapy. It is seen as a common factor accounting for therapeutic success (Bachelor and Horvath, 1999; Beutler et al., 1994; Lambert and Bergin, 1992). The rekindled interest into the common factors in the 1970s led to a number of important questions about the active ingredients of the therapeutic relationship, and so to the therapeutic alliance. The alliance was newly formulated to include the client and focus on the collaborative and interactive elements of the relationship (Bordin, 1979; Luborsky, 1976). Bordin has proposed a general definition that encompasses the bond between client and therapist, and the agreement on goals and tasks as the three main components of the alliance. A number of measures of the alliance have been developed. The Working Alliance Inventory (WAI: Horvath and Greenberg, 1989) was developed in line with Bordin's definition. Studies show that the therapeutic alliance is the single most important predictor of psychotherapy outcome (Orlinsky et al., 1994). The early alliance (third to fifth sessions) is particularly important in this regard. In the NIMH Treatment of Depression Collaborative Research Program already referred to, Krupnick et al. (1996) found the alliance to be a common factor across the modalities of treatment. The working alliance is a crucial ingredient in the therapeutic relationship. Clients and therapists tend to perceive the relationship differently, and it is clients' perceptions of the relationship that generally appear to be more relevant to outcome (Horvath and Symonds, 1991; Lambert and Bergin, 1992). More experienced therapists' evaluations of the relationship match more closely to those of their clients (Mallincrodt and Nelson, 1991).

The specific therapist responses that best foster a strong therapeutic relationship vary from client to client, and sensitivity to a client's differential responses is important. Tailoring the relationship to individual clients may be even more important than tailoring treatments to their disorders (Bohart et al., 1998). The therapeutic relationship itself can represent a therapeutic intervention, and may initiate change (Bachelor and Horvath, 1999; Bohart et al., 1998; Lambert and Bergin, 1992). For a review on the literature on the therapeutic relationship and the implications for practice, see Bachelor and Horvath (1999).

3 Hope as a psychotherapeutic foundation

This encompasses placebo and expectancy and has been unified by Snyder et al. (1999) into a theory of hope. It has long been recognised in medical research that the administration of pharmacologically inactive substances can have curative powers. This has come to be known as the placebo effect. Beecher (1955) concluded from his review of the literature that placebos produced 'satisfactory relief' for a variety of conditions, including post-operative pain, cough and headache. These placebo effects in psychotherapy literature are often called 'non-specific effects' or are controlled for. At first, psychotherapy imported the use of placebo control groups largely unchanged from the field of medicine. After some elaboration and increasing sophistication of the definition, disillusionment over the meaning and importance of the placebo in psychotherapy outcome research started to emerge (Critelli and Neumann, 1984; Kazdin, 1986; Wilkins, 1984). Frank and Frank (1991) argued that the effectiveness of placebos results from their ability to mobilise clients' expectancies for improvement. There is research evidence that the expectations that the clients bring to therapy have an important influence on therapy outcome (e.g. Frank et al., 1959; Tallman and Bohart, 1999). Clients have also been observed to experience significant improvement following an initial diagnostic interview or merely after receiving a promise of treatment. Therapists' expectancies may also play a significant role in therapy outcome. Hope is understood as how people think about goals. Frank (1973) observed that people come to therapy because of lost hope or depleted morale. Hope, in the model proposed by Snyder et al. (1999) has two components. These are the thoughts that people have about their ability to produce one or more workable routes to their goals (pathways thinking), and the thoughts regarding their ability to begin and continue movement on selected pathways around those goals (agency thinking). Both types of thinking must be present for a person to experience hope. The research suggests that an effective way to work with clients is to facilitate clients' hope through means of finding a new goal, a new pathway or a new sense of agency. The linkage between all three means the starting point can be geared to the needs of the client. It has been suggested that part of the therapist's effectiveness comes from modelling hope (Snyder, 1994; Snyder et al., 1997). Therapists can instil hope by directly communicating to clients both their hope for change and reasons for being hopeful. Conversely, there are common therapeutic practices that may lessen hope (Snyder et al., 1999).

4 Technique and model factors
There is debate in the literature as to how far research will go in the future towards the common factors, or finding more differences between different techniques. Details for specific findings related to techniques and models in the British literature can be found in Roth and Fonagy (1996). Some researchers anticipate that future research may reveal greater distinctiveness between approaches as the use of therapy manuals becomes more important and more frequently applied.

At this stage, it is certain that techniques like other common factors, contribute to positive therapy outcome. Specific techniques may provide an extra boost to change, depending on the client group. This is taken by some researchers to provide evidence against the common factors, and by others to complement the role of the common factors. For example, Lambert and Bergin (1992) state that unique or special variables may be important at times as well as the common factors and these are not mutually exclusive. Some authors have suggested that it is impossible to separate techniques from the common factors, as techniques can never be offered in a context free of interpersonal meaning within a unique therapeutic relationship (Butler and Strupp, 1986).

What do other sources of evidence contribute to our knowledge?

The voice of the client
The consumer reports survey reported by Seligman (1995) was a novel, but controversial, example of this. An American consumer organisation mailed 180,000 members with a questionnaire asking

if 'at any time over the last three years you experienced stress or other emotional problems for which you sought help from any of the following: friends, relatives or a member of the clergy, a mental health professional or a support group'. There were 22,000 respondents of whom 2,900 had seen a health professional. For this group of people, the longer the therapy, the better the outcome. This was shown for up to two years of therapeutic contact. No specific type of therapy was better than any other for any type of problem. This is a good example of incorporating client feedback in a naturalistic way. There has been widespread criticism of the research because of the lack of rigour in design in relation to conventional positivist methodology. This raises the common question about the relative meaning of statistical as opposed to clinical relevance of the results.

Developmental and affective neuroscience

There has been a recent movement within the field of neuroscience to integrate neurobiology with attachment theory, and theories of mind and the emotions. A large impetus for this has come from the interest of some psychoanalysts of making real Freud's prediction of a rapprochement between psychoanalysis and neuroscience. This research is now providing new ways of looking at psychotherapy.

Evidence from this relatively new field of affective neuroscience demonstrates how awareness of feelings develops in the primary attachment relationship between a mother (usually) and her baby. These early experiences have a decisive impact on the neuro-architecture of the brain, and on the nature and extent of adult capacities. Early interactions don't just create a context; they directly affect the way the brain is wired (Courchesne et al., 1994). Genuine synaptogenesis similar to that occurring during this period of neural plasticity (this refers to the potential for change) in early childhood can also occur in later life, during critical or sensitive periods. Studies throughout the 1980s noted the potentially plastic nature of the mammalian nervous system, demonstrating both 'experience-dependent' and 'experience-expectant' changes in neural structure and function (Greenough et al., 1987; Klintsova and Greenough, 1999). The ability of the brain to change structure and function (plasticity) is a prerequisite for long-lasting change in cognition, emotion and behaviour. Psychotherapy stimulates processes akin to brain plasticity (Liggan and Kay, 1999).

There is evidence for the role of psychotherapy in inducing real neurophysiological change. There is direct evidence that psychotherapy leads to neurobiological changes that can be demonstrated on brain imaging, in people with obsessive-compulsive disorder (Baxter et al., 1992; Schwartz et al., 1996). There are indications that functional anomalies in positron emission tomography brain scans are reversible by interpersonal psychotherapy as well as medication (Brody et al., 2001; Martin et al., 2001).

Neurobiological research is demonstrating the importance of emotion as a central organising process for consciousness. 'Emotions are the vital threads of value that run through the whole neural system' (Watt, 2003: 109). Antonio Damasio provides evidence that 'certain aspects of the process of emotion and feeling are indispensable for rationality' (1994: xiii). There is neuroscientific evidence (Schore, 2001) suggesting that it is helpful to become attuned (Stern, 1995) to our clients' expression of affect by means of our emotional imagination or empathy. Schore describes this process as affect regulating.

The results of the neuroscience research are thus in good accord with some of the overarching principles of humanistic psychotherapy in relation to the importance of the relationship and of the emotions in humanistic psychotherapy.

What conclusions have been drawn from the evidence for health policy?

This incorporates the focus on cost-effectiveness as well as that on change. There is a strong movement to evaluate the cost-effectiveness of the psychotherapies. There is considerable debate as to how much this is clinically driven, and how much this is economically driven. This is linked with the drive towards an evidence-based practice (EBP) paradigm. This movement started in the 1980s in hospital medicine, to promote better standards of healthcare interventions and to base health policy and management decisions on evidence of clinical effectiveness through a rigorous programme of research. As part of the strategic movement to apply research findings to the full range of psychological therapy provision in the UK, as part of the movement in evidence-based healthcare. In 1996, the first official policy statement on psychotherapy provision was published (the NHS executive review of strategic policy on psychotherapy services in England: Department of Health, 1996) together with the research review that had been commissioned to inform it (Roth and Fonagy, 1996). These two documents set the agenda for evidence-based psychotherapy in the UK. This model emphasises collaboration between researchers, clinicians and those commissioning services. The NHS executive policy review concluded that it goes beyond a reasonable conclusion based on the research evidence to list validated treatments at this stage. However, those responsible for commissioning psychological therapies should not fund services or procedures where there is clear empirical evidence that they are ineffective. Parry's caveat to her conclusions has important implications for humanistic and other integrative therapies:

> Formal psychodynamic and eclectic (type B) therapies have been insufficiently researched; the *absence of evidence for their effectiveness* must not be taken as evidence of ineffectiveness. (NHS Excecutive, 1996: 53, italics not present in original)

This situation is very different in the United States where similar developments, but in the service context of 'managed care', have led to an emphasis on 'empirically supported treatments' where criteria have been set for which forms of psychotherapy have good evidence of efficacy, and therefore will be funded by health insurance companies (American Psychological Association Task Force on Psychological Intervention Guidelines, 1999; Chambless, 1996). This is an important example of how two opposing conclusions have been drawn from the same evidence on each side of the Atlantic.

What other current trends are informing the evidence base of the future?

Psychotherapy research is currently in a state of transition. Orlinsky and Russell describe a current phase of 'consolidation, dissatisfaction and reformulation' (1994: 197). The concept of discovery, as opposed to verification of scientific fact, has once again come to the fore.

1 THE RECOGNITION OF THE IMPORTANCE OF CLINICAL SIGNIFICANCE The question as to what constitutes clinically meaningful as opposed to statistically significant change for clients is being addressed in both outcome and process research. A common criticism of outcome research using standard quantitative methods, or employing controlled clinical trials, is that the reporting of results of studies in terms of statistical significance may not illuminate how that research may be clinically relevant to a therapist reading that research and considering its application to a particular client or caseload of clients. Statistically significant improvements do not necessarily imply clinically important improvements for individual clients. For example, in a well-designed study, small differences after treatment between large groups could produce findings that reach statistical significance, while clinically there may be little difference between the groups in terms of symptoms or levels of adjustment. Jacobson et al. (1984) proposed using statistical methods to demonstrate recovery, or a change to a more healthy state of functioning. This change would be described as clinically significant. It is not always possible,

however, to identify an appropriate normative group or find a reliable way of measuring this type of change. It may not be possible to apply this type of definition to clients wrestling with existential issues, or in a process of self-actualisation, rather than in a 'dysfunctional' state.

2 THE RE-INTEGRATION OF QUALITATIVE METHODS INTO MAINSTREAM PSYCHOTHERAPY RESEARCH Qualitative methods have traditionally been considered as most appropriate for research which seeks to uncover meaning, and to contribute to the growth of understanding. Concepts from ethnography, linguistics, sociology and philosophy are increasingly being used and integrated. The integration of feminist methodologies has led to increased awareness of issues of empowerment and social responsibilities in research. There are many ways in which qualitative research can be done (see McLeod, 2001a). Case study research has played an important role in the development of therapy, and will continue to inform the development of future practice. A multiple case study approach has been suggested by Rosenwald (1988). Grafanaki and McLeod (1999) have carried out research on the use of narrative as a means of understanding the therapy process. Moustakas (1990) introduced a model of heuristic research as a way of investigating varieties of human experience. Rennie (2001) has reviewed the widening use of grounded theory in humanistic psychotherapy research (Glaser and Strauss, 1967; Strauss and Corbin, 1997).

Stiles (2001: 606–7) highlights some of the following distinctive characteristics of qualitative research that make it suitable for addressing humanistic topics:

1 Results that are reported in words rather than only in numbers.
2 Use of many descriptors rather than restriction to a few common dimensions or scales.
3 Use of investigators' empathic understanding of participants' inner experiences as data.
4 Understanding and reporting of events in their unique context.
5 Selecting participants or texts or other materials to study because they are good examples rather than because they are representative of some larger population.
6 Reports that use narrative or hermeneutic interpretations.
7 Empowering of participants considered as a legitimate purpose of research (e.g. encouraging them to change their social conditions).
8 Tentativeness in interpretations. The gain in realism can compensate for losses in generality.

Calls for methodological diversity and pluralism in research are becoming increasingly common (Howard, 1983; McLeod, 2000). However, according to Goss and Rowland:

a fully pluralist approach to evidence-based health care would draw on quantitative and qualitative methods, and the reductionist and phenomenological paradigms that underpin them, at all stages of the research process. The formulation of research questions, study design, data collection and interpretation, presentation of the findings and collation of these findings into systematic reviews would all have to satisfy the requirements of each approach. (2000: 201–2).

3 RE-ALIGNMENT OF THE GAP BETWEEN RESEARCH AND PRACTICE Many students of psychotherapy as well as experienced practitioners experience a gap between research and practice, and question the relevance of research as it is written and published for their practice. This is well-documented in the literature (e.g. Barlow et al., 1984; Morrow-Bradley and Elliott, 1986; Talley et al., 1994; McLeod, 2001b). There are many reasons for this. Researchers and clinicians may work with different priorities and different paradigms. It is often difficult for practitioners working with individual clients to understand the research, or to see the relevance of research in relation to their individual clients. Morrow-Bradley and Elliott (1986) carried out a large survey of therapists in the US – even though 88 per cent of the sample had PhD degrees, the source of information they found most useful was their ongoing experience with clients, supervision, the experience of being a client and practical books. They found these significantly more valuable than reading research articles or doing research.

It is easy to forget that the roots of psychotherapy research lie in individual clinical practice. As we have seen, the early literature was rooted in clinical practice and published by clinicians. After a long middle period where psychotherapy research has been largely carried out in academic institutions, or through larger-scale studies, there is a growing questioning of the relevance of some of these research questions to clients with unique identities as they present to psychotherapists in clinical practice. There is a growing movement to stop, slow down and look in more subtle and complex ways at what is happening in the relationship between practitioner and client. The practitioner and the subjective are back in focus in the research. The common factors researches, and the bridging research from attachment and neurobiology, are directly linked to clinical practice. Some of the qualitative methods, such as narrative analysis and case study research, are user-friendly for therapists who have no experience of research. The publication of the *Counselling and Psychotherapy Research* journal is a good example of the trend to reduce the gap between research and practice, with its emphasis on reflexive writing and fostering practitioner engagement in research.

One of the barriers that many therapists experience is the fear that the introduction of research interviews or questionnaires will interfere with the therapeutic process and be resented by clients. The evidence from clients suggests otherwise. Marshall et al. (2001) explored the subjective experience of clients who had participated in an outcome study of the effectiveness of psychodynamic psychotherapy. The majority of the clients found the experience slightly or moderately helpful in facilitating therapy. The therapists, by contrast, believed that the experience had been harmful to their clients. Berger and Mallison (2000) discuss several aspects of the therapeutic potential of research participation by clients. Madigan (1999) has reported a case where a client was invited to collect information about how others perceived him (through letters), and then use qualitative methods to identify the themes. Bischoff et al. (1996) have used time within narrative therapy sessions to collect information from clients on their appraisal of how things are going. Etherington (2000, 2001, 2002) has co-written a book with two of her own ex-clients, as well as editing the stories of counsellors and clients in rehabilitation and health settings. These examples represent new ways in which research can be integrated with practice.

> The research suggests that clients appreciate being asked their opinion; they feel empowered and value the opportunity to make a contribution to improved services for others. (McLeod, 2001b: 9)

This is compatible with the evidence that promoting client involvement is a key principle of empirically supported practice (Bohart et al., 1998).

The research informs us that client factors are the most important common factor and that good matching of client and therapist is important. The problem with the increasing trend towards evidence-based practice and the drawing up of guidelines, certainly within settings outside of private practice is that a type of paternalistic system may emerge where clients are given what is thought to be best for them. Education, class and personal finances and resources may become increasingly entrenched as a way of determining what choices clients have. Certainly if the research issues are complex for practitioners, one can only begin to surmise what problems clients might have in making informed choices. The research into the impact of involving clients in research is in its infancy. It makes intuitive sense that this might be a way of empowering clients and improving client choice.

If this seems a step too far, there are some small ways that practitioners can be involved in research. McLeod promotes the idea of seeing ourselves as a 'knowledge community' (2001a). Discuss and share your knowledge and experience with your colleagues. If you read something interesting or controversial, tell someone about it. If you are involved in research, consider whom you can work with. There are an increasing number of models of collaborative practitioner-oriented research (McLeod, 1999). Ask questions. The first principle of research is to have a good question, not to come up with any answers. If every practitioner took one step towards the research, what might the impact be? Further relevant information on psychotherapy research can be found in McLeod (2001a, 2003) and the following websites: http://www.talkingcure.com and http://www.psychotherapyresearch.org.

CRITIQUES OF PSYCHOTHERAPY

YVONNE LAWRENCE

The goal of psychotherapy is to alleviate human suffering and to facilitate individuals to realise their psychological and emotional potential. However, there are in many individual cases impediments to achieving these goals which lie beyond the scope or reach of psychotherapeutic endeavour. Human unhappiness is predicated upon a complex interplay between objective current environmental factors and subjective intrapsychic distortions or limitations to perception, affect and cognition, to a greater or lesser extent based on the individual's historical experience. It is specifically in this second subjective arena that psychotherapy is relevant. While a better functioning person may be more likely to effect changes in their environment which may in turn increase their level of satisfaction and happiness with life, it would be naïve if not dishonest to ignore that some human beings are by fate confronted with environmental problems much greater than their fellow human beings; in some cases greater to the point that the notion of personal responsibility and freedom becomes almost meaningless.

To discuss critiques of psychotherapy requires first an acknowledgement of the inherent limitations of the approach. Where human unhappiness is predominantly a result of poverty, social injustice, political oppression or social upheaval such as war, famine or economic collapse, psychotherapy has little to offer and what it can offer is only meaningful where accompanied by more direct intervention aimed at addressing immediate survival needs. For example, there is a growing initiative to provide psychotherapy for asylum seekers who have been traumatised by the horrors of war, political persecution including physical violence, torture and sexual assault. To offer this to someone without addressing their basic needs for shelter, safety and food, however, would be pointless.

There was a cartoon strip in a social work magazine some years ago which showed the social worker asking the harassed client, 'but how do you *feel* about your rats, Mrs Smith?' This graphically makes the point just as well for psychotherapy – sometimes it's Rentokil or the Housing Department who hold the key to the alleviation of human misery and psychological distress, and in these cases psychotherapy is irrelevant.

Furthermore psychotherapy is only ever as good as the psychotherapist offering it. Critiques of psychotherapy, to have any credibility, need to take this into account, recognising that the same broad range of skill level and instinctive talent is evident in this profession as it is in any other. While the profession can be held accountable for providing appropriate training, monitoring adequate standards and ethical practice, it should not be judged on the basis of individual therapeutic failures or therapeutic errors, whether of commission or omission. Mediocrity will always be part of professional practice in any field because practitioners do not all have the same level of intellect, commitment or, crucially in the field of psychotherapy, the same ability to relate to other human beings.

To shift focus from therapist to client, it is perhaps a bit clichéd but nevertheless true that clients only benefit from psychotherapy inasmuch as they are open to the process and willing and able to change. Perhaps the psychotherapist has some leeway in terms of inspiring or communicating hope to the temporarily hopeless, in encouraging and nurturing the seed of growth but there will always be individuals who do not want, for whatever reason, to take the risk, to feel the pain and here again we are presented with the limitations of the model. It cannot be done to the patient without their involvement and co-operation. Viewed in this way the limitation becomes a reassuring protection against abuse.

Because it falls so resoundingly between science and art, psychotherapy is that much more difficult to critique. What criteria for evaluation should we adopt when there is such breadth of understanding about what psychotherapy is, how it works and what its underlying principles and value bases are? Three major schools within psychotherapy – the psychodynamic, the humanistic/existential and the cognitive behavioural – have very different fundamental assumptions not just about how they operate but more fundamentally about what they are attempting to achieve. Are we critiquing from a perspective which has integration and the making conscious of the unconscious its major goal, or from a viewpoint which prioritises the realisation of potential, autonomy, self-actualisation and the making of personal meaning, or yet again from a position which holds adequate social functioning as its chief objective? When you add to this already shifting ground the subjectivity of the client's experience and their own unique and personal evaluations about what constitutes good or effective psychotherapy, the complexity of the whole issue becomes apparent. Any critique is as subject to bias and as inextricably bound up with the value base of the person who is doing the critiquing as the aspect of psychotherapy it scrutinises.

I have therefore attempted to tackle the task of overviewing critiques of psychotherapy by focusing on the source of the critiques. I identify five, admittedly overlapping, groups – the psychotherapists themselves; other professionals in related fields such as medical professionals, psychologists, etc.; people with overt political agendas as their main concern, e.g. sociologists, political activists, policy makers; those who represent popular culture through the media in conjunction with the general public, recognising that there is a dynamic interplay between these two which means they cannot be separated; and finally clients or users of psychotherapy services. By somewhat artificially creating these five categories I hope to be able to contextualise the range of critiques so that the value bases and agendas from which they spring will be manifest. Implicit in this is a simplistic attempt to critique the critiques as they are outlined.

Psychotherapist's critiques of psychotherapy

Perhaps the most famous or widely publicised critique of psychotherapy emerging from within the profession was Jeffrey Masson's *Against Therapy*, first published in 1989. He makes the overarching claim that

it is therapy itself that is at the core of the corruption I have described in this book. Every therapist, no matter how kindly and benign in appearance and behaviour, is sooner or later drawn into that corruption, because the profession itself is corrupt. A profession that depends for its existence on other people's misery is at special risk. The very mainspring of psychotherapy is profit from another person's suffering. (1997: 296)

One area which Masson had researched while still a practising psychoanalyst was Freud's reneging on his findings about the prevalence of sexual abuse in childhood and its impact on the psychological development of the victims (Masson, 1984). Masson charts Freud's subsequent revision and the development of his theory that women's reports of childhood sexual abuse were in fact evidence of 'an obscure internal area of confused desires and fantasies, a nest of unacknowledged needs, impulses, drives and instincts' (1984: 23) and he goes on to assert that this has become enshrined in psychotherapeutic practice. There is indeed debate and controversy within the profession about the extent to which a client's account of any event should be responded to as historical fact. Some would say the psychotherapist's legitimate emphasis is on the symbolic meaning of the account, or on its significance as a window into how the person makes meaning, or how their inner world of object relations is constellated.

Masson is also at pains to point out the danger of one set of individuals, namely the psychotherapists, claiming ownership of the knowledge and authority to understand and interpret the communications of another set of human beings, namely the clients, whose true meanings are hidden even from themselves. His concerns hinge on issues of power, hierarchy, dominance and 'rationalizations for abuse' (Masson, 1997).

There is a real philosophical and ethical issue here which psychotherapists undoubtedly need to address; namely the recognition that they benefit from the suffering of others and that this renders them vulnerable to unconscious self-interest potentially manifesting itself, for instance, in the promotion of dependency and even pathology in their clients.

While the danger which Masson identifies is real, it is by no means an inevitable outcome and can be guarded against by a culture of personal and political awareness and reflective practice among psychotherapists. We are not the only profession who make a living out of the suffering of other human beings and if he bases his call for the abolition and dismantling of psychotherapy on this argument, by the same token we must abolish and dismantle the medical profession, social work, the insurance business, the fire service to name but a diverse few of those who profit from suffering. Indeed it could be said that Masson has profited in no small way from his populist and inflammatory attack on the profession, his fame and no doubt financial success as a critic arguably surpassing his standing and success as a psychoanalyst. Holmes (1992) writes:

> Embedded in his invective are some valid and useful points, but he has delivered them with such violence that the psychotherapeutically minded reader has to make considerable efforts if he is not to respond in kind, and so dismiss Masson's whole project as the outpourings of a disappointed and unbalanced man. (1992: 29)

A final comment on Masson's critique in *Against Therapy* is that it relies heavily on highly selective examples of shockingly abusive bad practice to discredit the profession and is much less concerned with the more mundane nature of average or good psychotherapeutic practice.

Other more specific critiques of psychotherapy articulated by psychotherapists often reflect the author's modality in that they represent an analysis based on the theoretical assumptions of a particular school. As such it is often, although not always, discernible that the criticisms implicitly apply, at least more strongly, to philosophy, theory and methodology representative of a school of psychotherapy *not* practised by the author. To give some examples: R.D. Hinshelwood (1997), a well-established Kleinian psychoanalyst, in his book *Therapy or Coercion? Does Psychoanalysis Differ from Brainwashing?*, centres his critique of psychotherapy on what he sees as a flawed valuing of autonomy and assumption of rationality. His argument is that when the self of the client is split, projected or introjected, notions of informed consent no longer hold water and that the only legitimate and ethical role for the psychoanalyst is to foster integration. He goes on to demonstrate that such fostering of integration runs counter to any attempt to directly influence the client. Implicit in his argument is a criticism of what he terms 'suggestive therapies' whereby

> suggestion aims to override the patient's degenerate mental function by substituting the therapist's functioning ... Instead suggestion reinforces defences by diverting libido onto the physician and his suggestions – that is, his suggestions become sexually desired objects. (Hinshelwood, 1997: 132)

Hinshelwood's specific example of a suggestive therapy is hypnotism but his definitions as quoted here can clearly be applied to a cognitive behavioural approach:

> for example negative suggestion for the removal of specific symptoms or positive suggestion for best performance in specific events – the corrections invoked in the patient's thinking do indicate a special relation of the power of one mind over another ... In other words his 'internal' autonomy becomes dominated by an external authority. (1997: 133)

Interestingly this position could equally be seen to challenge certain tenets of humanistic and integrative psychotherapy practice which promote the notion of a developmentally needed relationship or the building of a healthier internal structure through reparative contact with the therapist.

Hinshelwood reasserts the role of abstinence whereby the therapist is careful to abstain from any form of self-disclosure, as well as the primacy of interpretation as the only legitimate form of intervention. These he regards as necessary safeguards against unethical practice and as prerequisites for genuine empowerment and integration. My point is that implicit in his critique of psychotherapy is the message that the only safe and appropriate psychotherapy is that which is firmly based on orthodox psychoanalytic principles.

A very different text which seeks to critique psychotherapy from a diametrically opposing theoretical stance and value base is Ernesto Spinelli's (2001) book *The Mirror and the Hammer: Challenges to Therapeutic Orthodoxy*. In this he argues that psychotherapy has lost its way because of its over-reliance on theories and models. He believes that not only does over-adherence to theoretical assumptions, accompanied by a highly specialised language and terminology confound and mystify the process of psychotherapy, but that this attempt to professionalise or aggrandise the profession paradoxically lays it open to criticism and scorn. He states that psychotherapy

has increasingly tended to become an ally of dominant cultural assumptions rather than one of culture's most trenchant critics. In so doing, it has puffed itself up in its pomposity and uncritical sense of its own self-importance. As a result, it seems to me that psychotherapy has encased itself within a set of restrictive interventions that doom its enterprise to a stagnant mediocrity which cannot be surpassed so long as it insists upon keeping the world out of the consulting room ... In this sense then, the once revolutionary possibilities of psychotherapy have given way to nothing more or less than the celebration of a self-servicing mediocrity. (2001: 18)

Ouch!

Coming from his own value base as an existential psychotherapist Spinelli elaborates upon his argument in ways which strike at the heart of psychodynamic orthodoxy, challenging the assumption of the unconscious as a core feature of human existence and questioning the legitimacy of the rule of abstinence and non-self-disclosure. However, his overview of the development of psychotherapy as a whole posits that in its loss of humanity, ordinariness and spontaneous contact between practitioner and client, therapy is not only limiting its effectiveness but the pervasive influence of psychotherapeutic ideas means it is having a negative impact on human relations as a whole. In making this point he quotes Emily Fox Gordon:

In the general progress of therapy, there was also a great and terrible loss of meaning. It was the realm of the interhuman that steadily shrank as therapy advanced ... The world we live in now is one in which nearly all of us ... are so thoroughly indoctrinated in the ideology of therapy that society has remade itself in therapy's image. To one degree or another, nearly every encounter looks like therapy now ... If therapy is all that we can give, or receive, then the possibility of mutuality has all but vanished. (2000: 228)

To demonstrate balance in making the point that psychotherapists across the major schools inevitably critique psychotherapy from their own theoretical perspective I need to mention the criticisms made most often by those of a cognitive behavioural persuasion; first regarding the lack of an evidence base for psychotherapy of other modalities (Roth and Fonagy, 1996). From the same quarter comes the challenge regarding the ethics and efficacy of long-term clinical work as practised both by psychodynamic and humanistic/integrative practitioners. On this point Elton Wilson writes:

> While humanistic approaches to psychotherapy are critical of many aspects of psychoanalysis, the notion of the 'length' of psychotherapeutic engagement as somehow indicative of its 'depth' is not usually challenged. Indeed it is an aspect of psychoanalysis that is held in somewhat reluctant awe. The emphasis on 'quantity' rather than 'quality', as the means to deliver conditions for true psychological change, has to be questioned and challenged by practitioners themselves if the profession is to withstand accusations of financial motivation and uncritical elitism. (1996: 7)

What strikes me as fascinating in these not just varied but frankly contradictory critiques of psychotherapy, so clearly embedded in the different theoretical orientations of the authors, is a strange similarity of tone and moral elitism. This is evident first in the assumption that what they are saying seeks to stem the tide of negative trends within psychotherapy as a whole. My own assessment of what they are saying is that rather than representing original challenges to the mainstream, they are retrenching into positions which have long been claimed and clearly articulated by the distinctly different schools of psychotherapy. Maybe the real questions they raise and the challenges they make concern the nature and credibility of integrative psychotherapy, a force which indeed represents a growing trend, if not in reality the mainstream, of contemporary psychotherapy.

A second fascinating similarity in these different discourses entails the assumption that the author's perspective is the ethical perspective and that it is the 'other' theoretical positions which pose a threat to the integrity of psychotherapy. Furthermore in the descriptions of these threats many of the same themes emerge over and over again, albeit from such seemingly different viewpoints. These themes seem to revolve around misuse of power and the deleterious effects of self-interest as manifest in therapists of 'other' persuasions.

This raises the consideration as to what extent self-interest and the normal human yearning for power have been denied by psychotherapists generally and are therefore condemned to be constantly recycled in the form of projections onto 'other' psychotherapists. However, this call to recognise the ubiquity of self-interest and hunger for power, to own it and reintegrate it into ourselves as psychotherapists and into the profession as a whole, is beyond the remit of this review of critiques of psychotherapy and therefore rests here.

Such diversity of critiques from within the profession itself, reflecting the multitude of different therapies, theories, philosophies and methodologies, in many ways attests to the dynamic and complex nature of the field. Change and growth are unlikely to emerge as the product of a culture of cosy consensus and fixed practices.

One of the clearest debates within the psychotherapy ranks at the moment revolves around the issue of whether increasing professionalisation and in particular mandatory professional registration of psychotherapists is constructive and part of a natural evolution or a destructive limiting movement which seriously undermines the creative nature of psychotherapy itself (Mowbray, 1996). Lomas (1999) concludes, echoed by Spinelli, that as psychotherapy enters the mainstream, therapists have become dependent on the technical, medicalised aspects of their profession and on the myth of neutrality in their dealings with clients at the expense of a more moral form of therapeutic human contact. As Lomas puts it:

> The respect for ordinariness diminishes with every new technique. Medical expertise has much evidence to justify its methods (although less than is commonly supposed) and the cultural impact of this fact puts increasing pressure on the therapist to think and practise under the guidance of a centralised organisation, rather than rely on the quality of their relationship with those who seek help. (1999: 138)

Critiques from related professions

I briefly turn to the criticism most often posed by professionals in related fields such as medicine and psychology, namely the lack of an evidence base and supporting research within psychotherapy.

Psychotherapy by its very nature does not easily lend itself to established research methods. This is due to the centrality of subjectivity within psychotherapy and the fact that agreed objective outcomes which can be measured are less clear in this field than they are, for example, within the context of medicine.

It is also therefore not surprising that the form of psychotherapy which finds most favour with the medical profession and attracts the most funding is the model which most closely reflects the medical paradigm in terms of subscribing to a view of a healthy norm – the form of psychotherapy referred to is CBT or Cognitive Behavioural Therapy. Cognitive Behavioural Therapy has furthermore traditionally been practised by, among others, psychologists employed in the mainstream who have built up a body of research data attesting to the success of the model in achieving quick (and thereby cost-effective), behavioural (therefore easily measurable) change.

Psychotherapy is in this context a relatively young profession in comparison with the more established medical profession or even psychology. These related professions have well-developed power bases with available funding for research into their own practice outcomes as part of their historical development. As part of the mainstream they operate largely within the public sector. As such they are in a strong position to shape definitions of efficacy and to set agendas with regard to objectives. Medical and social paradigms therefore dominate discourse about human suffering, and psychotherapy finds itself trying to work and prove itself within these less than compatible parameters.

Indeed in recent years a significant section of the psychotherapeutic community has embraced the challenge of finding ways of adapting research goals and methods to be more compatible with the values and practices of psychotherapy, e.g. grounded theory, heuristic research, etc. (McLeod, 2000; Moustakas, 1990).

In a fascinating article written for *The Guardian* Oliver James (2003) charts how over the last decade various research programmes, often undertaken by psychologists, have proven aspects of Freudian theory which have until recently been vilified and rejected by the academic psychology establishment: 'Advances in research techniques in the past 10 years had led to important findings that confound more than a century of rabid down-grading of Freud's status' (James, 2003). Freudian ideas which have more recently been validated in this way include the existence of transference phenomena, the prevalence of infantile sexuality in young children between the ages of three and six, and the claim that care or lack of care received during the first five years of life is more influential on adult outcomes than subsequent experience. The power of the unconscious and the significance of dreams have also been strongly supported.

What this appears to indicate is a coming together of the psychology establishment and the psychotherapy profession. However, a cynical psychotherapist's view of this is that psychologists with their research expertise, claim and market psychotherapy ideas more successfully and aggressively than psychotherapists themselves.

Research initiated in the field of neuroscience is another recent development to confer legitimacy on psychotherapeutic theory and practice, particularly in relation to the importance of attachment to the healthy development of the personality (Panksepp, 1998; Schore, 2003). It would seem that critiques questioning efficacy on the grounds of lack of evidence base are now more convincingly refuted.

A final comment placing the issue of evidence-based practice in a broader context concerns the fact that the same critiques have been levelled at other newer professions which challenge the supremacy particularly of the medical model. I refer to alternative therapies such as osteopathy and homeopathy which have also had to fight for their place in the established order.

Overtly political critiques

There are a number of varied criticisms levelled at both psychotherapy and psychotherapists which I will broadly group together under the heading of political critiques. This is not to suggest that the issues outlined elsewhere in this chapter are not political but simply to identify that political consciousness in its most overt form can be and has been directed towards a meta-analysis of psychotherapy as a social phenomenon. Such political analysis has emerged from diverse sources with equally diverse agendas, including philosophers, sociologists, politicians (both academic and policy-making), journalists and notably from psychotherapists themselves.

Indeed there is a move among some sections of the psychotherapeutic community to raise awareness of the interface between politics and psychotherapy and to espouse active responsibility for issues of social justice integrating them into the psychotherapist's agenda. This movement is evident in the formation of groups like Psychotherapists & Counsellors for Social Responsibility and in the work of writers like Pilgrim (1997) and Samuels (1993).

One of the recurring themes from critics such as Albee (1990), Cloud (1998), Epstein (1995), Pilgrim (1997) and Smail (1996) concerns the way in which psychotherapy obscures the origins of human distress through its emphasis on individual psychopathology. This argument proposes that psychotherapy also encourages people to focus their attention on individualistic notions of happiness and personal fulfilment, in ways which promote a capitalist agenda – the 'I'm worth it!' creed. Concepts deeply embedded in psychotherapeutic discourse such as autonomy, self-expression and self-actualisation can all lend themselves to the perpetuation of an ethic in which individuals prioritise their own private goals over any sense of the common good or community. Psychotherapy can be argued to have fostered the commodification of empathy, understanding or feeling for one's fellow human beings – these are now professional skills and qualities to be packaged, marketed and purchased.

This leads into the arena of the accessibility of psychotherapy, both in terms of who can afford it and who can relate to it. Issues of wealth/poverty, class, culture, race and gender raise their heads at this point. While short-term counselling is now more widely available on the NHS, largely through the growth of counselling in primary care, psychotherapy with its largely extended, intensive format and therefore attendant cost implications is much less widely available. It is in the private sector that there has been a proliferation of psychotherapy, which of course means that it is those who can afford to pay who have access to the services of psychotherapists. The charge emerges that psychotherapy is the preserve of the narcissistic, self-indulgent affluent.

Furthermore the criticism has been levelled that the jargonised technical language of psychotherapy renders it less accessible in other ways: this language and its value base are located in a white, Western, middle-class male view of the world, given that it was largely white European and American academics who developed the field of psychotherapy (Feltham, 1999). As such it can be experienced as alien and alienating by those who are not part of this dominant group or whose culture is based on different assumptions. For example, the heavy promotion of autonomy and personal identity as goals is at odds with a certain Eastern cultural perspective which has a much stronger emphasis on fulfilment arising from the person functioning as part of a social group with a shared identity. Another example would be the barrier presented to a potential client with a poor educational background and restricted linguistic repertoire by the reliance on sophisticated and abstract language as the primary form of communication in psychotherapy.

House (2003) goes further by suggesting that psychotherapy rather than freeing people from the shackles of redundant and unhelpful ideas, has simply created an alternative ideological framework and discourse, which is self-justifying, self-perpetuating and which limits the horizons of both client and therapist. To quote House:

> I maintain then that the very existence of profession-centred therapy as a culturally legitimate form of 'intervention' serves to create a socially and ideologically constructed 'regime of truth' which routinely constrains rather than liberates human experience, thereby bringing about the very opposite of therapy's professed intention – i.e. ossification rather than

organic growth change or transcendence ... Perhaps the commodified form taken by profession-centred therapy has been a necessary stage in the evolution of human consciousness and has served an important purpose. But what promised to be – and for many no doubt has been – a liberation has increasingly become a fetter which limits that very evolution. (2003: 15)

I think the challenge which House is making is a serious one in that he confronts the complacency and over-identification which inevitably arise when one works *within* any theoretical framework, particularly when one's professional status and livelihood become dependent on the maintenance of that frame. He challenges us to question as psychotherapists our own role with both individual clients and historically as a force within society as a whole. Does psychotherapy and do psychotherapists today really ally themselves with unpredictable but vital human potential – what might be – or do we from an unconscious position of self-interest and conservatism foster a culture of acceptance of what is – albeit accepted with greater equanimity and humour? At a societal level the question revolves around the extent to which psychotherapy represents a radical force for transformation and social change or to what extent it supports the status quo, regardless of its rhetoric of liberation.

We have only to look back at the figures and the battles which have dominated the evolution of psychotherapy throughout the twentieth century to see reflected the retrogressive developments identified by House. From Freud on, the founders of psychotherapeutic schools were iconoclasts, characters who dared to think beyond received wisdom: consider Jung, Ferenczi, then later Kohut, Rogers, Perls and Berne; their energy was often focused on confronting the orthodoxy of the mainstream. Today psychotherapists are largely preoccupied with *becoming* part of the mainstream, with *being* established and orthodox; hence the focus and energy directed towards greater professionalisation and registration.

Another different and even more disturbing analysis, skilfully explored and articulated in the BBC's television series *The Century of the Self*, was the view that psychotherapy was doomed from the outset to serve the capitalist agenda. No sooner had Freud proposed the existence of the unconscious than the earliest exponents of the advertising industry, including Freud's own nephew Edward Bernays, were using the concept to consider how they might better understand and shape the desires and unconscious motives of the public so that profits could be made from gratifying these same desires and motives. In the process needs became defined in terms of material goods, and the citizen, betrayed by his unconscious, became a good consumer. The programme went on to chart how the subsequent rise to prominence of a seemingly different philosophical and methodological manifestation of psychotherapy such as the humanistic school was inexorably shaped by and harnessed to the same capitalist agenda. Self-expression as a goal was easily moulded and eloquently achieved through high-profile consumption and possession.

Of course one would only need to look at psychotherapy from a politically right-wing perspective to come up with a completely different set of critiques. These might be focused on the inadvisability and moral degeneracy inherent in encouraging the expression of emotion and vulnerability, or on the perniciousness of advocating disrespect towards authority figures such as parents, with the claim that the consequence is a culture of blame. Perhaps the place where such critiques are most often found is in representations of psychotherapy within popular culture and within the media, to which I will now turn.

Media critiques of psychotherapy

In reviewing the core themes evident in negative media representations of psychotherapy what is most noticeable is not the originality of the criticisms but the hostility revealed in the language used, which in some cases borders on the vitriolic and inflammatory. I consider first the content and substance of a small selection of these critiques before commenting on the meaning of the tone and the interplay between media representations and the public view of psychotherapy.

One recurring media claim is that psychotherapy encourages people to engage in self-indulgent navel gazing, to approach the normal disappointments and vicissitudes of life with self-pity underpinned by unrealistic expectations of a perfect 'happy' lifestyle. Julie Burchill, in a column for *The Guardian* entitled 'The Whine Industry', writes:

> Too many people in the world today mistake disappointment for depression and believe that it is a problem to be treated rather than a fact of life to be lived with and worked around.

A second discernible theme concerns the pejorative portrayal of emotionally expressive behaviour, as encouraged by psychotherapists. Often when this issue is raised by the media it is done so in mocking 'humorous' terms; see, for example, a *Sunday Times* Leader dated 2 March 2003:

For too long Britain's quivering stiff upper lip has been showing signs of increasing tremor. Derided by touchy-feelies, psychologists, therapists and other head shrinkers, it has striven to maintain its traditional stoicism in the face of an avalanche of criticism. It has been told to quiver, to waver and to wobble. It has been told to let it all hang out and that nothing should be bottled up.

This article goes on to refer to new research which concludes 'that the people who deal best with tragedy and trauma are those who do not dwell on it. Talking about it just makes things worse'.

Julie Burchill in her 2001 column reaches further realms of mockery and derision making the same point.

Do we really have any solid proof that letting it all out is better than bottling it up? ... I'm reminded of the Monty Python sketch about the Pirhana brothers, Doug and Dinsdale, loosely modelled on the Krays. When an earnest young reporter reminds a sentimental old neighbour of the boys that they did in fact nail people's heads to coffee tables, she bursts out 'Well it's better than bottling it up, innit!' Is it? Look at the likes of Stan Collymore and Paul Gascoigne: total victims of the modern lie that expressing oneself, no matter how ugly the results, is preferable to exercising a little self-control.

Such articles frequently express concern at what they see as the proliferating number of psychotherapists; using terms like '*swarms* of therapists' (Tavris, 2003, emphasis added) or 'the *army* of counsellors who now outnumber the real British Army' (*Sunday Times*, 2003, emphasis added). The rhetoric is reminiscent of right-wing expressions of repugnance and fear at what they see as an invasion of immigrants and asylum seekers. This fear is presumably a fear of otherness which threatens to alter familiar landscapes and ways of doing things.

It can in some cases lead into a form of ugly prejudice in which the integrity and very character of the feared other (be they psychotherapists or asylum seekers) is questioned and reviled. Burchill (2001) sums this up in her description of therapists as 'carpet-bagging parasites' who spread 'enervating slime throughout society'.

A less lurid but equally hostile attack was made by Carol Tavris in the *Times Literary Supplement* (2003). In it she crudely juxtaposes two books and ostensibly reviews them, in the process making damning allegations about the practice of psychotherapy. She champions the argument of Richard J. McNally who in his book *Remembering Trauma* apparently dismisses the notion of repressed or dissociated memories of trauma as 'a piece of psychiatric folklore devoid of convincing empirical support'. Tavris polarises the argument by dismissing Linda Caine and Robin Royston's book *Out of the Dark* (a client and therapist's joint account of a therapy in which repressed memories were surfaced) as perfectly illustrating 'every false assumption, cliché and misunderstanding about the mind and memory'.

Her aim in the article is to demolish the credibility of psychotherapy on the grounds that psychotherapists make generalisations, lack a scientific base for their practice and fall back on denial in the form of a self-justifying theoretical framework based on little more than anecdote and faith. More measured versions of these same concerns have been expressed by psychotherapists themselves and by academics in related fields, many of whom have been referenced in this chapter.

What Tavris also alludes to is the whole emotive area of false memory and the allegations directed at psychotherapists, social workers and medics that memories of traumatic events, particularly abuse, have been created and implanted by the interventions of professionals. What is significant here are not so much the issues she raises which are hardly original, but the potential impact of such a piece given the audience Tavris is writing for. Many readers may have little context or knowledge of the field of psychotherapy and may therefore be subject to influence without the counterbalance of other input. The media shapes attitudes and prejudice within the population at large (as well as reflecting them) much more extensively, and therefore effectively, than academic publications.

Let me now briefly consider why psychotherapy should attract such powerful and emotive criticism from the media. My own view is that the answer lies in an understanding of the role of psychotherapy within society as a whole. A profession which sets out to contain and transform the darker side of human nature sets itself up for attack. You could say it draws the fire of the angry, the rebellious, the envious, the dangerously wounded. You can't play in the mud of the human psyche without getting muddy. Furthermore, we all want heroes and villains to simplify things and on whom we can project our inner conflicts. It is the stock in trade and raison d'être of the media to provide the public with just such simplifying black and white narratives. Of course there are occasions, in the public consciousness, when psychotherapists, with the mystique of their craft, could conceivably become the heroes, who might magically find the answers one cannot find for oneself, and who might make it all better. Inevitably, however, the weight of such expectation cannot be borne by any profession and at that point of disillusionment psychotherapists will once more revert to being the objects of disappointed attack. The media launches such attacks on behalf of the public who pays the wages of its journalists and to what extent it either fashions and generates criticism or reflects the criticisms of its readers can never truly be disentangled or measured.

Users of psychotherapy – their critiques

The criticisms voiced by clients themselves form the final strand of this chapter. These criticisms range from accounts of gross boundary violations such as sexual abuse and exploitation through to more subtle, arguably iatrogenic side-effects of psychotherapy itself.

There are two distinct kinds of problem here; first the problem of therapists who at worst seriously lack personal integrity and at best lack judgement, skill and personal containment. These therapists exploit their clients in very obvious ways, perhaps sexually or maybe financially. This phenomenon has not been written about so frequently by clients themselves, possibly because of issues of shame and exposure, but organisations such as the Prevention of Professional Abuse Network (POPAN) testify to its prevalence. Those individuals involved with investigating and addressing complaints for professional psychotherapy organisations will be only too familiar with such examples but clearly the protection of the client requires that identities are not disclosed and that details are withheld from the public domain. However, the issue of therapists' sexual exploitation of clients has been written about by theorists – e.g. Hetherington (2000), Pilgrim and Guinan (1999), Russel (1993), Rutter (1990) – rather than by clients themselves.

The second kind of problem referred to has been written about by clients themselves and centres not so much on the lack of integrity of individual therapists but on negative aspects of the psychotherapy experience itself – see, for example, Alexander (1995), France (1988), Fox Gordon (2000) and Sands (2000).

A number of common themes clearly emerge from these texts: first a belief that psychotherapy sometimes created problems for the authors rather than solving them (France, 1988: 30–1). Alexander goes so far as to say, 'The personal difficulties that led me to therapy were dwarfed into insignificance by what was happening in the therapy itself' (1995: 91). She also claims that 'I did not suffer from the aberrant condition described in the book before encountering the therapist and have not done so since recovering from the experience' (1995: 17).

Even where improvements are noted, how is it possible to prove that these are a result of the therapy rather than attributable to other factors (France, 1988: 234)? Furthermore, France makes the point that clients who describe therapy as having been beneficial may be justifying their significant investment in the process by attributing their improvement to it: 'One does not want to have spent all that time and money for nothing' (1988: 27).

Doubts about whether psychotherapists actually know what they are doing are expressed by Alexander, who wonders whether psychotherapy 'knowledge was about as far advanced as medicine at the time of Hippocrates: a minimum of fact, a number of wild theories and a great deal of groping around in the dark, doing far more harm than good' (1995: 98).

Perhaps the most recurrent theme was the claim that psychotherapy fosters dependency. France described feeling 'abjectly dependent' on her therapist (1988: 30) and Alexander even more powerfully documents the experience:

> often I felt like a tetraplegic, utterly helpless and totally dependent but with no one to be dependent on – a state which induced panic. My 'self' seemed to be continually hovering on the brink of disintegration. (1995: 86)

She recounts how 'My life was wholly impregnated with Luc [the therapist] and an independent existence was no longer possible' (1995: 116).

On this point of dependency France makes some interesting challenges, questioning the psychotherapeutic orthodoxy that dependency is a stage on the road to autonomy (1988: 52). She also queries the ethics of inviting such potentially overwhelming dependency via the promotion of transference when the therapist knows that his reciprocal commitment has limits, for example he needs breaks and holidays.

The area of transference raises a myriad of concerns for these authors. Is the concept sometimes used to discount the actual experience of the client created by the therapy situation itself, rather than by the past (Sands, 2000: 133)? France certainly believes that transference is artificially caused by the therapeutic frame and setting, and believes that there is inherently 'excessive focus on the past and on fantasy to the detriment of present reality' (1988: 78). The frighteningly powerful experience of transference with its seductive quality is likened by Alexander to taking drugs, 'intoxicating, addictive, hallucinogenic and destructive' (1995: 1).

Both Alexander and France recount how their functioning in the world was in their view compromised by the experience of psychotherapy:

> Increasingly I felt that 'reality' concerned my sessions of psychotherapy while 'real life' became merely an intrusion ... I became much less able to cope with things ... I became unable to enjoy any of the activities I have previously taken pleasure in, unable to eat, unable to do anything creative. (France, 1988: 30)

Alexander's account is tellingly similar:

My activities in the real world had almost come to a halt. I was so perturbed by the experiences I was going through that it was virtually impossible for me to communicate socially. (1995: 55)

They both also testify to the enormous difficulty encountered in extricating themselves from the process of psychotherapy and making an ending. France emphasises the personal dilemmas of not knowing when to quit:

Rationally I felt I should stop therapy ... Emotionally I couldn't bear to abandon this one hope of security and improvement ... I had invested too much energy in the process and become too attached to my therapist to quit. And the more I hung on, the more incapable I seemed to become of leading a normal life. (1988: 31)

Alexander focuses more on the therapist's dismissal of her attempts to end therapy as evidence of her pathology. She is clearly angry that the therapist never considered the possibility that the therapy was not working. House, in his analysis of these same texts, makes an interesting hypothesis:

might therapy not typically be setting up an institutionalised co-dependency relationship, from which once established, it often becomes very difficult for either client or therapist to extricate themselves? (2003: 169)

These texts highlight a number of specific psychotherapy techniques and assumptions which the authors found alienating and unhelpful; this includes the therapist's redefining of a client's opinions, or even the client's objections to a particular therapeutic intervention, as further evidence of their pathology (Alexander, 1995: 53; Sands, 2000: 56). France identified both the therapist's use of silence as traumatising and the deliberate use of 'systematic frustration in the professional encounter' (1988: 229) as deeply untherapeutic. The therapist's conscious withholding of information about himself is another issue raised, and on this point Alexander says: 'Of course if something is hidden people want to know what it's all about. It's enough to drive people insane even if they're not crazy already, (1995: 87).

Sands makes the point (2000: 34) that the very concept of the unconscious puts great power into the hands of the psychotherapist whose job it is to interpret it as they see fit, while disempowering the client and weakening her 'faith in the validity of all our judgements and perceptions'. Implicit in this criticism is the charge of infantilisation. Furthermore the therapist may see in the client what his training has told him to look for (2000: 42). On a general note Sands objects to the way in which psychotherapy accentuates pathology and encourages clients to identify with labels rather than locating and promoting what is healthy and functional (2000: 87).

One of the important issues which Sands addresses is the danger inherent in the process of psychotherapy that the problems and unresolved issues of the psychotherapist can become projected onto the client (2000: 140), thereby compounding and further obscuring the nature of their distress.

Yet another issue highlighted by both Sands and France and one which quite rightly often preoccupies psychotherapists themselves is the difficulty entailed in judging when a client has the personal resources to abandon defences which may have enabled them to function, and when they have not (France, 1988: 237). France poignantly identifies a conundrum, namely that the dangers of psychotherapy are greatest for the vulnerable individuals who need it most (1988: 240). Her own personal experience was that enhanced personal awareness and insight in themselves did not improve her general well-being:

> all it did was reveal a lack of something important in my childhood which had not been remedied by adult life. Knowledge of this need did not appease it, but on the contrary made it obsessive and destructive, since I no longer seemed to be able to function efficiently in other spheres because of my crippling sense of emotional deprivation. (1988: 199)

What she is here illuminating is the dark possibility that some clients rather than resolving early trauma may through the process of psychotherapy simply relive them and be retraumatised (1988: 32). Sands succinctly poses the challenge: 'How confident can practitioners be that their clients will always work through, rather than simply relive, early emotions and experience?' (2000: 131).

Such direct accounts of personal experience make for uncomfortable reading. Clearly there are clients who do not meet with sufficient containment, empathy or skill to help them successfully transcend and transform their pain and there may also be a small minority who enter the process unconsciously or consciously determined to see it fail them. However as psychotherapists we have much to learn from the reflective observations of those who have been on the receiving end of our services. Who better to guide us about what we do and how to do it? To quote France, we need to

> shift from the idea that this is a treatment meted out by a specialist to a sick person, who has no right to question it, to the attitude that this is a co-operative venture between two equals, with the same goal of effectively enhancing the life of the consulter. (1988: 243)

Final comments

Critiques inevitably raise anxiety in those whose theory and practice are being critiqued. However if psychotherapists can stay open enough to embrace what these critiques have to offer, the whole profession of psychotherapy has a better chance of remaining healthy whilst continuing to develop its useful role within society. If we defensively close our ears to the words of our critics we will become increasingly marginalised and eventually stagnate. To quote Colin Feltham:

> Non-defensive, responsive interest in critiques is likely to ignite the kind of curiosity needed to maintain the relevance, or change the shape, of psychotherapy ... in rapidly changing times. (1999: 308)

We have to balance such openness alongside a realistic awareness that critiques sometimes emanate from sources whose motives are tainted by competition, envy and desire to monopolise the intellectual, financial and status conferring potential of psychotherapy. Such motives apply in particular to certain critiques articulated by psychotherapists themselves and those in related professions. Furthermore psychotherapists can be subject to unfair and destructive attack by wounded, vengeful individuals or by those working in the media who enjoy finding objectives for their invective and making entertainment and money out of doing so.

This presents us with the challenge of staying in dialogue with our critics, from a position of integrity and curiosity with a genuine desire to reflect and learn, while maintaining our belief in the essential value of psychotherapy (after all, there is at least as much evidence of the efficacy of psychotherapy, much of it from clients themselves) and having the intellectual and moral robustness to withstand attack.

Challenging although this may be, it is useful to recognise that it is exactly what is demanded of clients in the process of psychotherapy. They are also invited to deconstruct the very nature of their own identity, to question their strategies and ways of being, in a process that is often experienced as painful, shaming and disorientating. The expectation is that throughout this process they will have the courage and willingness to remain in contact with the therapist who represents a source of critique, albeit we hope a constructive and empathic one. The parallel speaks for itself – if we believe it is worthwhile for clients to subject themselves to such scrutiny, it must be worthwhile for psychotherapists to do the same.

5

PSYCHOTHERAPY IN THE NHS

TRICIA SCOTT

The state of the nation's mental health

According to the Department of Health, at any one time one adult in six suffers from one form or other of mental illness (DoH, 1999a). The figures vary depending on how 'mental illness' is defined and the kinds of emotional distress that are included. A distinction has been made between mental 'distress' which affects daily living, 'mental disorder' which means an impairment of functioning which affects self or others, and 'mental illness' which conforms to a recognisable pattern and may be diagnosed as a discrete category of illness according to the American Psychiatric Association's *Diagnostic and Statistical Manual of Mental Disorders* (APA, 2000).

Records in psychiatric services of 'mental illness' that include psychotic episodes such as schizophrenia and the affective disorders provide the most accurate figures, and these report a fairly stable figure of under 1 per cent of the adult population who suffer this kind of severe mental illness.

Estimates of the prevalence of 'distress' and 'disorder', on the other hand, are more difficult to calculate. Goldberg and Huxley's research (1992) found that about one-third of those presenting in primary care suffer from 'non-psychotic anxiety and depression'. This figure does not include those suffering distress that is sometimes called 'psychosocial', nor those whose emotional problems relate to illness such as cancer, heart disease or diabetes, nor the so-called 'psychosomatic' complaints such as eczema, irritable bowel syndrome and asthma.

According to government figures the number of people, particularly young men, committing or attempting suicide have significantly increased in recent years, as well as those who self-harm or suffer from eating disorders, those who misuse drugs and alcohol and the elderly with mental health problems.

These figures are for the adult population. However, the World Health Organisation offered a warning in 2003 that the fastest growing mental health problem in the world, particularly the developed world, was among adolescents. A longitudinal study of 15-year-olds over three generations provides evidence of this in Britain. The research, published in 2004 and funded by the Nuffield Foundation, was conducted by the Institute of Psychiatry, Kings College London and the University of Manchester. It shows that the mental health of teenagers has sharply declined in the last 25 years, with the rate of emotional problems such as anxiety and depression increasing by 70 per cent amongst them.

There are therefore large numbers of both adults and young people for whom an appropriate psychotherapeutic response could make a significant difference to the quality of their lives. There is also increasing evidence that a psychotherapeutic response is effective in facilitating this change (Roth and Fonagy, 1996). At the heart of the situation is the question of whether this response should be provided from the public purse and on what grounds a person may gain access to this kind of help.

The nation's mental health and the state

It seems that the government is taking this challenge seriously. A number of government initiatives have highlighted mental health as a priority, including the White Paper 'Saving Lives: Our Healthier Nation' (DoH, 1999b), which has mental health as one of its four key areas, and 'Modernising Health and Social Services: National Priorities Guidance' for 1999/2000 and 2001/02.

The 1999 National Service Framework for Mental Health encompasses all aspects of mental health, from mental health promotion through to continuing care and changes in the way mental health services are organised. The care and aftercare of those suffering mental illness has historically been provided through the health committees of the local health authorities and this has meant that there has always been a problem of inequalities between regions and uneven distribution of services. The general bias towards hospital matters in the administrative structure of the NHS meant that the community-based services, essential for mental health, suffered neglect and underpinned inadequate local liaison between hospital and community staff. A succession of legislation from the 1959 Mental Health Act onwards has supported the move from hospital-based mental health services to care in the community, but this has until now been inadequately supported by financial investment and the organisational structure of the NHS.

In 1997 the Department of Health's White Paper 'The New NHS' introduced Primary Care Groups and Trusts (PCTs), putting primary and community services at the heart of the NHS. These were a key part of the drive to improve health and address inequalities. PCTs are 'free standing statutory bodies with new flexibilities and freedoms responsible for delivering better health and care to their local population' (NHS Executive publication, 'Primary Care Trusts: Establishing Better Services', 4/99). They have taken on many of the functions of the health authorities, such as commissioning services and investing in primary and community care. They can also directly provide a range of community services, creating new opportunities to integrate primary and community services, as well as improving mental health provision.

Primary care is the coal-face of the health service, including mental health services. Some GPs say that emotional and psychological issues are a factor in up to 90 per cent of the people they see (Scott, 1994). As someone who has set up and run a primary care psychotherapy service, I am strongly aware of the number of people wanting and needing psychological help and the severity and complexity of the problems they present. I understand too that publicly funded services have financial constraints and there must be sound ways of assessing people's needs and safe, efficient and effective ways of responding. However, it seems as if there is great anxiety that unless access is controlled the floodgates of distress will open and services will be inundated. There seems to be a parallel process between the individual's fear of their own or others' distress becoming overwhelming and perhaps leading to 'madness' and this need for control.

Mad, bad or dangerous to know?

Issues of mental health are subject to cultural and social attitudes and economic conditions. Mental illness, disorder or distress can be frightening for the sufferer and for their family, friends and others. It can become confused with criminal behaviour, dangerous behaviour or behaviour that is a nuisance or threat to public order. Within the various debates about whether debilitating states of distress are based in physiological, psychological or environmental factors – nature or nurture, chemistry or genes, mothering or social conditions – lie further issues of moral judgement and social control. There are still many who regard mental illness and distress as indicators of a person's lack of moral fibre – the 'no backbone' and 'pull up your socks' brigade. There is still social stigma attached to a diagnosis of mental illness that may have an impact on employment chances, insurances, care and contact with children. Diagnostic categories are used to allocate resources in public spending between mental health services, the justice system and as a form of social control whereby those who are considered a danger to themselves or others can be isolated from society.

Despite this, the care and treatment of people suffering mental distress and illness reflects a history of increasing understanding and social compassion. The cruelty and ridicule common in earlier times has gradually been reformed by more humane attitudes, endorsed by the state. As early as 1792 the 'Retreat' was founded in York by the Quaker William Tuke. Tuke was able to demonstrate that a caring and compassionate approach produced better results. The Lunatics Act of 1843 and the Lunacy Act of 1890 established the first coherent national policy to provide asylums for the mentally ill. Originally these were to offer protection for the mentally ill themselves. It was later that the emphasis became the protection of the public, and these themes are still in evidence today driving the mental health agenda. By 1930, with the passing of the Mental Treatment Act, treatment rather than custody was encouraged. Nevertheless by 1948, when the NHS began, mental hospitals were overcrowded and standards of living in them were very poor. Locked wards were the norm and comparable to prisons, with regimented daily routines (Levitt and Wall, 1992). Even today there is too much emphasis on containment and not enough on developing appropriate treatments (Scott, 1995; Mind, 2004; SANE, 2004).

The provision of services addressing the mental health of the nation and of prevention of illness, including mental illness, has always been a central part of the NHS agenda. Sir William Beveridge's central assumption in his 1942 report was the idea that a comprehensive system of healthcare was essential to any scheme for improving living standards. To him 'comprehensive' meant treatment available for every citizen as and when the need arose both in the home and in hospital. In the words of the 1946 National Health Service Act, the aim was to promote 'the establishment in England and Wales of a comprehensive health service designed to secure improvement in the physical and mental health of the people of England and Wales and the prevention, diagnosis and treatment of illness'.

Gradually over the years a succession of legislation has shifted the emphasis from compulsory detainment in hospitals to care in the community. In the mid-1950s there were still over 150,000 people in mental hospitals. The 1959 Mental Health Act reduced the numbers compulsorily admitted to hospital and this, with the developments in drug therapy, started a gradual reduction in hospital numbers. The 1962 NHS Plan predicted the closure of a substantial number of the older, isolated hospitals to be replaced by smaller units attached to the District General Hospital (DGH).

The 1975 White Paper 'Better Services for the Mentally Ill' also set out provision for more facilities in the community, and consequently day hospitals, sheltered work and adequate home support were all expanded. If people were ill enough they were to be admitted to the local DGH or if old and mentally infirm to the community hospital. Staff ratios were to be improved. These plans turned out to be not financially viable and many of the proposals were abandoned. Secure units, for example, were proposed for each region but most of these have still not been built, partly because of staff opposition or failure to agree on the type of patient who should be accommodated.

The Mental Health Act of 1983 placed greater emphasis on the rights of patients and gave health authorities greater responsibility for safeguarding these rights. Concerns of mental health professionals at that time centred on the overuse of residential, in-patient care in hospitals and secure units. The thrust was towards greater use of community treatment orders and the rights of patients with mental illness to a normal life in the community.

Now the pendulum has swung the other way and shortages of psychiatric beds mean that there is a danger that community orders will be used as a safety valve for overcrowded wards and be applied to patients who cannot be managed safely outside hospital. Mental health campaigners have expressed doubt about the discharge procedures. Under NHS guidelines patients with severe mental illness should have a care plan agreed on discharge from hospital that sets out the care and rehabilitation to be provided, identifying an NHS or social services worker co-ordinating care and specifying what action should be taken in a crisis. The guidelines are less rigorous for voluntary patients than those sectioned under the Mental Health Act.

A survey conducted by the charity SANE found many cases where patients had been allowed to walk off psychiatric wards after threatening suicide or harm to others without aftercare arrangements being put in place (SANE, 2004). The charity Mind is to publish a survey suggesting that a climate of fear and hostility exists on the wards. According to Mind, mixed-sex wards are still the norm and there is an over-reliance on untrained agency staff. For some patients support in the community is not enough. More recovery and rehabilitation accommodation and aftercare homes are needed to replace those that were lost when the large mental hospitals with rehabilitation homes in their grounds were sold off. At the time of writing, the government is setting out proposals for a new mental health bill. The issue of detaining people who may be a danger to the public is driving these current proposals. The government is attempting to put in place legislation that will allow for the detention of people diagnosed with 'dangerous personality disorder' who have never previously offended. Compulsory powers are proposed when three mental health professionals, including two psychiatrists, believe that this is 'clinically appropriate'.

However, the Royal College of Psychiatrists has expressed concern that a large number of people will be detained unnecessarily (*The Guardian* letters, 11 September. 2004) and by this are perhaps admitting the lack of certainty in the diagnostic tools available to them. 'Personality disorder' is a particularly controversial diagnosis. It has been used as the diagnosis for those patients who do not seem to respond to available psychiatric treatment and therefore are deemed 'untreatable'. On these grounds they can be refused access to psychiatric services (Scott, 1995; Parry and Richardson, 1996). There is clearly a need to develop more complex understandings, diagnostic tools and treatment, as well as to manage risk to self and others.

Re-defining mental health and illness

Currently people suffering emotional and psychological distress and seeking help from a trained professional in the NHS are assessed for mental health services on the basis of models of mental illness and disorder that derive from the medical concept of disease.

There are various systems of classification of mental illness and disorders. The World Health Organisation's tenth revision of the 'International Classification of Diseases' (ICD-10) includes a classification of mental disorders in its fifth chapter. A simpler version of this classification, for use in primary care and general medical settings, called ICD-10 PHC, includes advice on the management of the disorder (WHO, 1992). The *Diagnostic and Statistical Manual* of the American Psychiatric Association, now in its fifth revision (*DSM-4TR*), provides another classification that tends to place more emphasis on clear operational rules for making diagnoses (APA, 2000).

DSM-4 defines a mental disorder as a

clinically significant behavioral or psychological syndrome or pattern ... that is associated with present distress (eg a painful symptom) or disability (ie impairment in one or more important areas of functioning) or with significantly increased risk of suffering death, pain, disability or an important loss of freedom.

The definition states that syndromes or patterns must 'not merely [be] an expectable and culturally sanctioned response to a particular event, for example the death of a loved one' (APA, 1994: 23).

The problem with this definition is that behaviours that may be regarded as normal in one culture may be seen as aberrant in another. Distress and other symptoms are subjective, and clinical judgement is central in deciding whether impairment in functioning constitutes a disability. Who decides what the important areas of functioning are? In the psychiatric mental state test, for example, the tester assesses sleep and eating patterns and makes an assessment of 'healthy' social and intimate relationships, including a person's capacity to work and provide financial support for themselves and family. These are inevitably highly subjective assessments imbued with the social and cultural assumptions of the tester. What constitutes a significantly increased risk and on what basis? Many believe that the subjective nature of the diagnostic process leaves too much room for social and cultural prejudice and error. For many years, for example, homosexuality was regarded as a mental disorder and was categorised as such in the first and second versions of the *DSM*. It was eventually revised and appeared in *DSM-3* as 'Ego-dystonic Homosexuality' (APA, 1980). It was only as recently as 1987 that it was completely removed as a category in *DSM-3R* (APA, 1987). Research has shown that a higher proportion of individuals from black and ethnic minority groupings compared to the majority white population are diagnosed with mental illness such as schizophrenia (Harrison et al., 1988). Strong links have been found between poverty, class and social conditions, and depression and suicide (Brown, 1996; Gomm, 1996).

The disease model implies that a clear distinction can be drawn between normal or healthy and abnormal functioning, yet these notions imply norms and no norms have been established for either. In particular there is no clear line between those who are mentally and psychologically normal and those who are abnormal or mentally ill (Bentall, 1992: 33). Traditionally a line was drawn in psychiatric conditions between those that were defined as 'neurotic' and those that were 'psychotic'. Recent research suggests, however, that it is difficult to discriminate between normal and psychotic experiences (Kinderman and Cooke, 2000). Psychotic symptoms are often the severe expression of traits that are present in the general population. Suspicion of others' intentions towards us can shade into paranoia and in its severest form becomes paranoid delusions. There is evidence too that a large proportion of the population has had some kind of psychotic experience such as hallucination in their life (Bentall, 1992; Kinderman and Cooke, 2000).

To address the difficulty that 'what may be regarded as mental illness or disorder shades insensibly into normality' (Kendell, 1996: 24), the most recent thinking about mental illness proposes a continuum model. In this model what is deemed to be normal functioning is at one end of the scale and full-blown clinical psychosis or 'psychoticism' is at the other end, with shades of eccentricity between them. Using this continuum, researchers such as Kinderman and Cooke (2000) calculate that severe and debilitating distress or anxiety affects a huge proportion of the population. There is also evidence that some people may have recurring episodes of 'psychoticism' while others may only ever have one episode. Episodes can be severe or mild. They can be expressed outwardly in what is termed 'florid' behaviours or inwardly in deeply withdrawn behaviour.

Many complex and interacting factors are now thought to be involved in the development of states of distress that become unmanageable or symptoms of mental illness such as psychosis. These include biological, genetic, social and environmental as well as psychological factors. The APA describes its own use of the term 'mental disorder' as unfortunate in implying 'a distinction between mental disorder and physical disorder that is a reductionist anachronism of mind/body dualism' (APA, 1994: 21). Kendell says that 'neither minds nor brains become ill in isolation' (1996: 24). A further refinement to the continuum model is the stress-vulnerability model. This suggests that both biological and psychological factors may leave some people more vulnerable to environmental stressors and the development of more severe states of distress (Kinderman and Cooke, 2000). Brown has said that 'life events are the very phenomena that our brains have evolved to deal with. What happens in the outside world can have profound biological implications' (1996: 43).

The role of medication – pros and cons

There is little doubt that many people suffer personal anguish that is so severe and debilitating that they feel they cannot manage it on their own. Currently neuroleptics or anti-psychotic drugs, and lithium in the case of mania, are the main treatments for those suffering distress that includes psychotic episodes. These drugs do alleviate symptoms, and although much has been written about debilitating side-effects the subjective experience of psychosis can be very frightening or even life-threatening for the person experiencing it and a cause of great distress to family and friends. The drugs can be helpful in reducing psychotic symptoms and regulating a person's emotional state, even though little is known on a cellular or molecular level about how or why they work (Kendell, 1996: 260).

Clearly medication has a role to play in alleviating distressing symptoms. However, critics of the psychiatric focus on identifying disorders point out that pharmaceutical companies have a stake in psychiatric diagnosis and, for example, provide substantial funding to the APA's activities. A medical diagnosis invariably results in treatment involving drugs (Kutchins and Kirk, 1999).

Gabe (1996) says that the history of psychotropic medication has gone in cycles. As new drugs are introduced as safer and inducing less dependence, the rise in prescribing begins anew. Currently psychotropic medication is on the increase for people presenting with all levels of distress. More than 1 in 50 adults takes mood-altering medication permanently and 1 in 10 men and 1 in 5 women will take them at some time in their lives (DoH, 1999b). The pharmaceutical industry has historically disguised the risks to maximise profits. There is evidence of limited curative effects and dangerous side-effects and even the newest anti-depressants (SSRIs) need careful monitoring and are not a long-term solution. Their side-effects and withdrawal symptoms can be as severe and distressing as the original depression (Pilgrim and Rogers, 1996; CITA, 2002).

Integrating psychotherapy into NHS services

Some have argued that the medicalisation of distress may undermine individuals' sense of mastery and their contact with their own self-regulatory and self-healing capacities. It leads to the person thinking of themselves as a victim with little control over themselves, their behaviours and their destiny, and contributes to a culture of dependency.

Psychotherapy seeks to address the complexities of a person's experience and work with them to regain a sense of authorship of their own life. This might mean facilitating their confidence and ability to take charge of their own mental, emotional and physical states, including their medication and other forms of support that they feel they need to help them achieve this. Research shows that for many a combination of medication and psychotherapy is the solution that best addresses not just the symptoms but the causes and the management of distress that has become debilitating (Roth and Fonagy, 1996).

Psychotherapy can play an important role in bringing psycho-therapeutic insights into the medical arena. The medical profession has been moving towards more complex understandings of the holistic bases of health and disease – for example emotional and spiritual resources have been shown to have a profound impact on a person's capacity to heal (Goldberg, 1990). Models that integrate the biological, psychological and social elements involved in disease are being developed all the time. In particular the predominantly physical approach to psychological perspectives is changing, with evidence from neuroscience and infant studies suggesting a much closer connection between mind and body than has conventionally been considered to be the case (Scott, 1996, 2004).

In the NHS the term psychotherapy is used to cover a range of 'talking therapies' offered in primary, secondary and specialist ter-tiary settings. Most psychotherapy in the NHS is provided by staff who offer it as one component of a range of skills and as one com-ponent of a package of care. In Parry and Richardson's strategic review of psychotherapy services for the Department of Health (1996) they highlighted the different staff, both medical and non-medical, 'doing' psychotherapy in the NHS. These included psychiatrists, clinical psychologists, social workers, educational psychologists, child psychotherapists, art therapists, community psychiatric nurses and nurse specialists. According to this review, many of these professionals use a range of psychotherapeutic tech-niques pragmatically, rather than undergoing a full psychotherapy training in a particular school or approach.

Psychotherapy is poorly understood and there is often confusion between the school or theoretical approach of a particular psycho-therapy, between counselling and psychotherapy and between the different professions that bring a psychological understanding to their treatment response such as psychiatry and psychology (Scott, 1995).

The historical and professional roots of these different disciplines have led to different ways of thinking about the nature and causes of human distress, and as a result very different approaches to treatment have been developed. This can sometimes mean that the different responses to a particular person and their problem can be working against each other. A client who is starving him or her-self, for example, is likely to have their food intake measured and controlled and their weight checked by nursing staff in an eating dis-orders unit. A psychotherapeutic response may be to explore with the client the meaning for them of their control of their food intake. It may possibly be an expression of their lack of control in other emotional and psychological areas of their life, and the psychotherapeutic work may focus on the client regaining a sense of their own authority in both of these areas and in this way remove the need for disordered eating. It is important to be clear when one approach is more suitable in a particular case than another and that the different disciplines seek to understand each other's contribution and work together.

Mental health services in Britain are led by psychiatrists. Psychiatry is a branch of medicine and has mainly focused on the organic bases of human distress such as chemical imbalances in the brain or physical lesions. The result has been the categorisation of distress into various disorders and treatments following the disease model. Treatments offered by psychiatrists are still mainly pharmacological or surgical. Electro-convulsive therapy (ECT), for example, is still widely used in Britain and its use is on the increase within the NHS (Kendell, 1996). It is only recently that a basic exposure to core psychotherapeutic interventions has become mandatory for membership of the Royal College of Psychiatrists (RCP, personal communication, 2002). According to Parry and Richardson's review of psychotherapy services (1996), only 90 of 4,550 psychiatrists had completed a specialised training in psychotherapy, qualifying them for the post of Consultant Psychiatrist specialising in Psychotherapy in the NHS, although these have an important role in providing training and supervision to others.

The Chair of the Psychotherapy Faculty of the RCP confirms that this figure has not changed much since Parry and Richardson's review was published (Knowles, 2005). There are now approximately 145 posts for Consultant Psychiatrists in Psychotherapy in the NHS but many of these are part-time. The RCP currently only formally recognises three modalities in psychotherapy, CBT, psychodynamic and systemic, although it seems there are only one or two psychiatrists trained in systemic therapy. Despite this, new consultant posts must now be advertised generically and although the Chair considers that it remains a 'threatened specialty' for psychiatrists there are 2,000 members of the Psychotherapy Faculty who support the provision of a range of psychotherapies in the NHS.

It has been a long, slow process incorporating non-medical treatments into the mental health services. For many years clinical psychology in the NHS was a measurement discipline ancillary to psychiatry. It has developed into a therapeutic profession but this history is evident in the training and practice of clinical psychologists.

The emphasis in psychology has been on research into how humans grow and develop in normal circumstances and the British

Psychological Society (BPS), founded in 1912, fostered scientific interest in psychological treatment. The emergence of behaviourism as a theoretical force in the 1940s had a profound influence on psychological treatments, as during the 1950s and 1960s theories of learning, derived from animal experimentation, were applied to humans, bringing experimental methods to human psychological processes. In the NHS early work by Skinner and Wolpe was influential at the Maudsley Hospital and the Institute of Psychiatry, its sister organisation. By the 1960s behavioural treatments were available in many mental health services throughout Britain, focusing on the behavioural manifestations of distress as deviations from normal functioning.

The 'cognitive revolution' in academic psychology during the 1960s was followed by new emphasis on the cognitive processes in therapy. Cognitive principles were incorporated into behavioural therapy, and Cognitive Behavioural Therapy (CBT) began to be applied to depression, anxiety and other kinds of mental distress, including psychosis. CBT is still by far the most widely used form of psychological intervention in the NHS.

The term psychotherapy was first used in the 1890s by van Eeden and van Rentergen in Holland and was defined by them as 'the cure of the body by the mind, aided by the impulse of one mind to another' (Ellenberger, 1970: 765). Psychotherapeutic theories and methods have developed mainly from case studies of adults and children in distress and undergoing treatment. Their focus has been clinical observation, the subjective experience of distress and the underlying, often unconscious, psychological mechanisms involved. Early treatments were mainly psychoanalytic and the Institute of Psycho-analysis was founded in 1919. The Tavistock Clinic, founded in 1920, made these treatments available to NHS patients in London after 1948.

In the early 1970s there was an explosion of 'new' psychotherapies, partly as a result of the perceived limits of behaviourism and the rigidity of psychoanalytic thinking. These had their roots in the work of such diverse thinkers as Reich, Moreno, Perls, Maslow, Rogers, Berne and Kelly, and some were influenced by the existential philosophies. These approaches offer a way of thinking that is less about alleviating the behavioural symptoms of distress and more about facilitating self-regulation. They seek to facilitate the fulfilment of a person's potential, rather than the adaptation of their behaviour to a norm. They largely developed outside the NHS in the 'human potential movement' but have had an important influence in the development of the 'client-centred' ethos with which the NHS is now imbued. Gradually more of these approaches have become available in the NHS and applied to a wider range of problems.

In the last ten years or so there has been much cross-fertilisation and the differences between the various professional disciplines are shading into each other – partly as a result of the work of the United Kingdom Council for Psychotherapy (UKCP), the umbrella body that represents the full range of psychotherapies and the professional disciplines involved in delivering psychotherapy available in Britain. Interest in pan-theoretical and integrationist theories has burgeoned and in the underlying principles and common factors of all effective therapies that transcend theoretical schools. Psychological theories and understandings inform an important part of most psychotherapy trainings, particularly theories of human development and change. Research is now on the curriculum and many training organisations are linked to universities and offer Master's degrees in conjunction with the clinical training. A wider range of psychotherapeutic methods have been incorporated into the training and experience of clinical psychologists and psychiatrists. A special-interest group has been established in the British Psychological Society for psychologists who wish to specialise in psychotherapy.

The role of counselling in the NHS

Counselling is also widely available in the NHS. In the NHS counselling has come to mean a brief intervention of between 6 and 12 sessions, focused on managing a particular emotional issue or life event in the present and with clients whose difficulties are deemed mild to moderate. Clients are usually assessed as suitable for counselling when they do not have histories that indicate deep-rooted and entrenched difficulties in managing their lives and relationships (Burton, 1998). The level of entry to counselling training is usually at undergraduate level, as opposed to postgraduate level for psychotherapy. The training is normally shorter – two years part-time as opposed to a minimum of four years part-time in psychotherapy. This has financial implications for services, but may also distort the picture.

The reality in practice is often different. Many clients seen by counsellors are suffering severe distress. It is not always possible to identify at the outset those who may have long-term and deep-rooted problems beneath their current issues, and once a good therapeutic relationship has been established it can be anti-therapeutic to finish prematurely by referring on to someone else. More serious aspects, such as a history of sexual abuse, eating disorder or self-harm may not be revealed until some time after this relationship has been established. It is with clinical experience that a practitioner becomes able to accurately assess when it is appropriate to give more time and space to allow a person's feelings and thoughts to emerge or when and how to close them down. It is also a sophisticated task to establish a viable therapeutic relationship with a person who has developed powerful defensive strategies to cope with unbearable feelings, and to be able to contain and engage with a person's intense distress effectively.

How training prepares practitioners for NHS work

Over the last ten years in Britain the member organisations of the UKCP have been developing and refining training standards for psychotherapy, both generic standards for practitioners of all approaches and specific requirements that reflect the philosophical and theoretical assumptions of the different approaches. We can say therefore that what qualifies a psychotherapist as fit to practise has been established by discussion and agreement between all those, or the majority of those, already in the field.

Psychotherapy as recognised by the UKCP is a postgraduate training of a minimum of four years part-time, although most humanistic and integrative trainings are considerably longer than this, often involving six to nine years. The emphasis is on ensuring that a person is ready for independent practice of both long- and short-term therapies and is able to manage a varied caseload by the time they qualify.

The minimum curriculum requirements outlined in the training standards of UKCP incorporate many aspects that would be considered essential for work in the public sector and a survey of UKCP registered practitioners revealed that a significant percentage already work in some capacity within the NHS (UKCP, 1996). The UKCP guidelines regarding equal opportunities and intercultural practice commit psychotherapists to 'working towards an understanding of the meaning of cultural diversity' including 'fundamental differences of age, sexual orientation and abilities' and to acknowledgement of the 'impact of different cultural experiences on themselves, their clients and their work' and 'the reality of discrimination and prejudice in society as a whole and within the profession'. These guidelines become essential requirements for practice within the multicultural context of the NHS.

Many UKCP training programmes prepare trainees for work in the public sector as an integral part of their training and others include specialist modules for those trainees who wish to develop their careers in this way. The UKCP committee for psychotherapy in the NHS has developed guidelines for training in NHS practice (UKCP/NHS, 2002). A more in-depth focus on and critical understanding of diagnostic systems of mental illness and psychopharmocology is recommended as well as 'knowledge of current NHS policies, structure and systems and their implications for psychotherapy practice'. Clinical work in the NHS involves working under medical supervision and with the intensity of more severe psychological disturbance, and the guidelines place special emphasis on this. The assessment of clients' needs and the formulation of appropriate interventions, taking account of available and often time-limited resources in NHS contexts, are also priorities. There is a focus on learning to work in a multidisciplinary team, managing the pressure of large numbers and a wider diversity of clients. Knowledge of the legal, ethical and administrative frameworks relevant to NHS practice is also essential. These training guidelines were developed in line with the Counselling and Psychotherapy Forum for Primary Care's recommendations for primary care specific trainings (CPForumPC, 2001).

However, many of the values of the recent government policies for mental health are already embedded within the ethos of psychotherapy. Client-centredness is a key theme running through these initiatives and a central concept particularly in humanistic and integrative psychotherapy approaches, where the client is understood to be the expert regarding their own lives and problems. Psychotherapy trainees learn to establish collaborative working relationships, conduct in-depth conversations with clients based on empathic understanding and trust, and listen to and understand subtle and complex layers of communication. Notions of lifelong learning are an integral part of the culture of psychotherapy, encapsulated for example in the ongoing practice of supervision and continuing professional development. The emphasis is on personal therapy and ongoing commitment to development of self-awareness and reflective practice, attending to one's own vulnerabilities and needs as part of the commitment to ethical practice.

How psychotherapy fits with evidence-based practice

Central to the government's initiatives regarding mental health is the concept of 'clinical governance'. Clinical governance offers a framework through which NHS organisations are accountable for continually improving the quality of services, and ethical practice and evidence-based practice are important aspects of this. I believe that research into the effectiveness of psychotherapy is fundamental to ethical practice and that we owe it to our clients to be able to demonstrate that what we are doing is safe, effective and efficient, whether we are working privately or in a setting funded by public money (Scott, 2004).

Roth and Fonagy were commissioned by the Department of Health to undertake a review of all the available evidence regarding the effectiveness of psychotherapy (1996). They found good evidence for the effectiveness of a range of psychotherapies in many mental health problems, including severe and enduring mental illness.

In the NHS interventions are commissioned on the evidence-base of their effectiveness. Evidence-based healthcare (EBH) is an international drive that began with evidence-based medicine (EBM). EBM is defined as 'the conscientious, explicit and judicious use of current best evidence in making decisions about the care of individual patients' (Sackett et al., 1996).

In medicine the best available evidence is usually based on the outcomes of systematic research. The randomised controlled trial (RCT) is described as the gold standard of systematic research in medicine, and the systematic appraisal of results from these trials is now an established feature in many areas of healthcare.

RCTs are experimental designs that attempt to establish scientifically clear relationships between cause and effect by controlling the variables. In RCTs of psychotherapy interventions, 'subjects' or clients are chosen who have a matching diagnosis of a discrete category of problem such as 'depression' and are then randomly assigned to various treatments or placebo groups. Data that indicates change is collected and ways of measuring this change established. Attempts are made to reduce any contamination of the major variables, including trying to ensure equity in therapist competence and to standardise treatments. The results of RCTs are subject to statistical analysis (Herbert, 1990).

However, the emphasis on RCTs as the underpinning of evidence-based practice of psychotherapy is problematic. RCTs were developed to test the effectiveness of medical interventions where it is easier to isolate and control the variables. Psychological processes cannot be separated in the same way. It is difficult for example to gather a sample of clients for a controlled trial that is representative of those seen in routine practice. The notion of discrete categories of problems is suspect as discussed earlier, and most clients, particularly those seen in the NHS, have complex and multiple problems. The usefulness or 'external validity' of such research to practitioners is therefore reduced to the point of being meaningless.

A further problem with RCTs is that in order to control the variables, efforts must be made to standardise therapeutic procedures by controlling the duration of the therapy and by using manuals that specify the parameters of the interventions the therapist can use and exactly how the therapy is to be conducted. However, outside the research setting such adherence to a pure formula is not only rare but can be argued to be anti-therapeutic. Individuals are unique and skilled therapeutic responses involve engaging with this uniqueness. A therapist makes choices about how to respond to the particular client and their needs at any given moment in the therapeutic relationship. To specify a formulaic response denies the client that very quality of responsiveness that many believe to be one of the significant factors in the healing process.

Randomisation is also problematic. It removes the client's choice and this is an important part in the process of therapy. The government's policies emphasise collaboration with clients in negotiating goals and their preferences for treatment approach and therapist. These are inaccessible to research using RCTs. In the current context of healthcare the call is for 'unbiased, relevant and reliable assessments' (Chalmers, 1998). However, the issue of bias is endemic in psychological research particularly. There is growing evidence for example that differential outcome effects between psychological therapies can be attributable to researcher allegiance (Robinson et al., 1990; Gaffan et al., 1995).

Statistical methods are not necessarily helpful when transferred to individual cases. We do not yet know nearly enough about why some clients do better with some therapists and in some therapies. Practitioners may find it useful to look to research that focuses on therapeutic process. The RCT is not the best way scientifically or economically to address process issues.

There may also be dangers in an over-reliance on evidence-based practice. Parry warns that valuable and effective therapies may become unavailable and creative innovation damaged if research is used to drive public sector funding and cut services and costs rather than inform practice (Parry, 2000).

Keeping in mind the reservations outlined, there is nevertheless reasonable evidence of effectiveness from RCTs on a range of therapeutic methods with common presenting problems such as anxiety and depression. Roth and Fonagy (1996) also point out that the fact that just because there is no evidence of effectiveness of a particular approach does not mean that it is ineffective.

Practice-based evidence

A distinction has been drawn between 'efficacy studies' such as RCTs and 'effectiveness studies' which are conducted in a routine clinical setting. The term 'practice-based evidence' has been coined to highlight this distinction and current thinking in the field stresses the importance of both in the case of psychological treatments in the NHS.

The evidence for psychotherapy can be drawn from many sources, including detailed descriptions of cases, systematic observational studies, process and process-outcome linked studies, longitudinal studies of patient series and non-randomised outcome studies (such as case control studies). Qualitative interviews can enhance and complement quantitative data, such as large sample surveys of psychotherapy recipients and process research.

Barkham and Mellor-Clark (2000) have emphasised the need to investigate psychotherapy as it is actually delivered, where the effects of self-selection, patient preference, therapist competence, service delivery context and referral patterns will all be present. In RCTs these are all considered to be confounding factors, but they are all important factors in effective therapeutic process. The kind of studies that focus on routine clinical practice are called observational and descriptive research rather than experimental, but have an important role to play in furthering our understanding of what we are doing.

Barkham and Mellor-Clark recommend the establishing of Practice Research Networks (PRNs) to create an infrastructure to support effectiveness research. The PRNs would take a naturalistic approach to utilising data gathered in routine practice settings rather than clinical research trials. All practitioners would use the same clinical measures and data collection tools, which would generate large data sets and permit comparability between client populations, interventions and services. CORE (Clinical Outcomes in Routine Evaluation) is one such system now widely used in general practice to monitor effectiveness, help identify continuing professional development (CPD) needs of therapists and help service managers monitor and compare the contribution of individual practitioners to service performance.

Conclusion

Our understanding of the nature of mental ill-health and well-being has changed dramatically since the birth of the NHS in 1948. The idea that it is shameful to experience emotional problems is slowly on the decline and gradually people are becoming more willing to acknowledge their emotional difficulties and seek professional help. We can no longer rely on firm distinctions between those who are considered mentally ill and those who are healthy or normal. The emphasis is shifting towards listening and responding to people's own accounts of their needs and experiences. There is also growing recognition of the importance of the emotional, psychological and spiritual aspects of a person in their physical health and well-being. Numerous studies have shown for example that a cancer patient's emotional and spiritual resources can have an impact on the rate of their tumour growth and their survival (Goldberg, 1990). At the same time the range of interventions and responses found to be helpful has also increased. Major advances in psychotherapeutic treatments during this time have been fostered by the NHS and are increasingly reflected in NHS provision.

The NHS Plan outlined radical change in the way the NHS is organised (DoH, 2000). In 1996 about a third of general practices either had a designated counsellor in the practice or direct access to counselling services. The Primary Care Trusts, introduced in 1998, are now required to ensure that all general practices in the group have fair and equitable access to a range of psychological therapies commissioned on the basis of an assessment of the population need.

The aim is to place the needs of patients before those of what the government calls the 'professional tribes', with the emphasis on teamwork and services depending on the skills of staff, rather than job title. They believe that for too long traditional demarcations between staff was holding back the progress of the services. Changes in medical training have included the introduction of a common foundation programme for all healthcare professionals and since 2002 all practitioners have had to show an ability to communicate with patients in order to qualify.

Hopefully these changes will begin to create more flexibility in the system so that appropriately trained and qualified psychotherapists can be employed and resources made available to fund further research into what works for whom and how. Beveridge's vision of a health service that offers to every citizen access to services when the need arises may yet become a reality for those whose needs are emotional and psychological.

6

TRAINING FOR A CAREER IN PSYCHOTHERAPY

CHRISTINE LISTER-FORD

Training to be a psychotherapist is an intensive and demanding undertaking. Not only is the trainee required to gain a theoretical grasp of a subject that is both fascinating and complex, they must also be able to apply their learning effectively with their clients. Unusually for most professional trainings, the trainee psychotherapist must come to know themselves at least as well as the theories they are studying; generally by undertaking their own personal therapeutic journey of heart, mind and soul. There is a straightforward reason for this. The chief instrument for most psychotherapists is the self. Their own thoughts, feelings and reactions provide the main means of assessing, judging and understanding the efficacy of the work. Even where other tools are used to aid assessment (such as standardised tests) they do not obviate or replace this use of self. This is because psychotherapy is essentially based on relationship, even where the methods used are mainly cognitive, behavioural or hypnotherapeutic. The effective practice of psychotherapy is a well-blended synthesis of art, science and reflection. Psychotherapeutic practice is a multidimensional activity, which requires both objectivity and inter-personal sensitivity.

It follows, therefore, that to be able to use oneself well there must be clarity of personal knowing. The demands on the student to attain this are great. And at its most challenging this training can make one feel that there is no place to hide from scrutiny; either from that of others, or from one's own. It takes courage, determination and fortitude to pursue this career path. At best when personal transformation, enjoyment of learning and mastery of skill are harnessed and flowing in tandem, students feel all the passion, pleasure and excitement of a journey which has revealed rare and wonderful vistas that outmatch any prior expectation or imagination. Although students often experience the polarities of the pleasure and difficulty of this training, they are rarely bored or uninterested!

Personal qualities needed in a psychotherapist

Personal maturity

Training to become a psychotherapist is not normally a first career choice. The personal qualities required to understand other people in the context of their own lives mean that a psychotherapist must have maturity derived from a depth and range of personal life experiences. They must know the ups and downs and the joys and pains of life. The three regulatory bodies for psychotherapy in the UK take a range of views about the minimum age at which training can commence. The United Kingdom Council for Psychotherapy requires all trainees to be 25 years old before they commence training. The British Association for Counselling and Psychotherapy has no minimum age requirement although many diploma courses recognised by the BACP do individually set down 25 as a minimum age. The British Confederation of Psychotherapists comments: 'The BCP is a regulatory body for its member societies and a register. As such we would obviously not have a minimum age requirement' (e-mail communication, 18 August 2004).

Any minimum age limit is at the discretion of the individual training organisations. The minimum length of training varies from three to four years according to the regulatory body. The European minimum, set down by the European Association for Psychotherapy, is four years. This means that by the point of graduation most psychotherapists have a minimum age of around 30, although many of course may be older.

Sensitivity and the capacity for self-reflection

Beyond the bare minimum of age-related maturity, a psychotherapist needs to have a personal style and approach that is sensitive. The capacity to attune empathically to a client's feelings, experience and perception is essential. This is straightforward when the material the client brings evokes a sympathetic response. But it can be much harder when the client's story provokes problematic or negative feelings for the psychotherapist. At such times a therapist needs the ability to put their own judgements and preferences aside and to see things from the client's point of view. Achieving this requires personal self-reflection, and the ability to use one's own responses as a barometer by which to reach a greater understanding of the client's world. In such circumstances, the psychotherapist needs robust means by which to process their own emotional responses so as to understand what in their reaction is triggered by their own history and what in their reaction may be a normal part of how the client tends to impact others. Typically during the training phase, personal psychotherapy, together with guidance from one's supervisor, are the usual ways of working through and understanding problematic emotional responses to the client.

A genuine interest in other people

A genuine interest in others is an obvious prerequisite in a psychotherapist. However, what is accepted as 'genuine' at the social level is not what is meant by 'genuine' at the psychological level. Socially, helping people by giving advice, wanting to make someone feel better, wanting to stop someone feeling lonely – these are all valuable and important. They smooth social relating, give comfort and do genuinely help alleviate distress. The psychotherapeutic journey is not, however, a social undertaking. For the client it is usually a combination of alleviating distress and gaining greater clarity of perception about what has created personal difficulties. To achieve this, people have to be prepared to feel their pain, to know where it originates and to look at ways in which they, themselves, can either alleviate it or come to terms with it. These therapeutic goals cannot be achieved if someone steps in to make things better by smoothing them over or trying to take them away.

So for the trainee psychotherapist, motivation to work with others must be carefully examined and understood. The student of psychotherapy needs to be sure that they want to assist through therapeutic and not social means. Of course, everyone meets some of their own personal needs through the work. This is both a legitimate and necessary outcome. Like every other professional, a psychotherapist needs to enjoy their work, feel good about what they do and feel personal esteem and satisfaction from their endeavours. Alongside this, the therapist must be satisfied that they are avoiding the obvious 'bad' reasons for practising – filling an emotional void in their own life, wanting to help others 'see the light', or meeting a personal need to be needed.

Training components

Postgraduate study of a core profession

Psychotherapy is a postgraduate-level activity. Alongside the right personal qualities, candidates need to have a proven ability to study at a higher level. Generally speaking either a relevant first degree, or prior training and/or work with others in a helping capacity is essential.

In mainland Europe and North America students are required to have a so-called 'core profession' in either medicine or psychology before they are eligible to practise psychotherapy. This requirement has had the effect of limiting training opportunities for those without these prior qualifications and has been hotly contested, especially in Europe, as an unfair, restrictive practice. Perhaps the greatest benefit to derive from this approach, however, is that by limiting training to those with conventional 'helping professions' backgrounds the public are sometimes better protected from charlatans and unprofessional practice. Certainly, as we will see in the next chapter, many of the arguments about professional regulation and how to ensure psychotherapists are rigorous in their practice have been avoided by this approach, where acquiring psychotherapeutic knowledge and skill is seen as a specialism or development of one's existing abilities and knowledge.

In the UK the training of psychotherapists and the provision of psychotherapy have not been controlled in this way so the profession is open in principle to any suitable candidate. Psychotherapy is viewed as a core profession, even though it is not regulated by statute. The lack of regulation (as we will see in the next chapter) causes confusion about the status and standing of psychotherapists and can sometimes lead to unscrupulous practice by those with little or no training who are still, at the moment, allowed to call themselves a psychotherapist. Out of the lack of regulation two loose 'camps' have emerged within the profession.

- those whose practice is based in a range of settings such as private practice, or part-time in primary care settings within the NHS
- those within secondary care in the NHS who tend to corner the market in full-time paid posts as psychotherapists because of their initial training as a medical doctor or clinical psychologist

At times there can be a clash of views between these 'camps', particularly about who has the right to own the title, speak out on issues and gain rightful recompense. Where these debates take place they are generally rooted in issues of power and control and driven by a desire to establish ownership. Those who work privately often have greater freedom of practice once they have established themselves. But becoming established is initially harder. Practitioners often have to show through the quality of their work that they have had a proper training which has fully equipped them for practice and that they are not part of the 'flaky fringe'. It can be irksome to have to do this, but it is best to know the reality of the professional world and be ready for it.

Therapeutic skills

As a vocational training, the study of psychotherapy requires the student to develop the skills that mean they can put theory into practice in the consulting room with their clients. It is not enough to be academically competent; the trainee must be able to translate their abilities into tangible interventions that can produce effective therapeutic movement. This aspect of the training, together with personal psychotherapy, takes the longest to master because it is dependent on understanding relevant theory, being able to appraise its significance for a client, and then being able to formulate the right intervention.

Supervision

Supervision of client work is vital. In working so closely with someone it is easy to lose perspective or to overlook something that someone more distant from the relationship would see as important. Initially, the supervisor is there to monitor and assess the efficacy of the student's work and to ensure they are working safely within the limits of their competence. As the student gains expertise the supervisor's role changes and they become more of a consultant and mentor, someone whose advice, knowledge and expertise is valued and sought out to help in retaining clear understanding.

Supervision throughout one's professional life as a psychotherapist is a requirement of many accrediting organisations and most modalities. It ensures there is always someone external to the therapeutic relationship to consult with about any problem areas.

Personal psychotherapy

Alongside theory and practice the student will usually pursue their own therapeutic journey, following the same twists and turns of the path that they will expect their clients to follow. There are some notable exceptions to this norm – family therapy and cognitive behavioural therapy where the modalities themselves make it difficult for a student to pursue a course of therapy via them. For example, with family therapy the student would need to persuade their entire nuclear family to take part. Gaining this kind of consent is not always possible or, indeed, desirable. Students learning these therapeutic modes are not usually expected to take their own therapeutic journey. In my view, it is nevertheless still desirable that they do so, by undertaking a course of personal psychotherapy in a related modality. The inner journey of the therapist is invaluable in providing a felt understanding of what it is like to be in the client's shoes.

Without having placed oneself in that position it can be easy to misunderstand what it is like to make oneself so exquisitely vulnerable to another human being.

Most courses specify the minimum requirements for a therapist who will provide psychotherapy for a candidate in training. The therapist would normally practise the modality being studied by the student, and either be very close to qualification themselves or already have qualified.

Courses also specify the minimum hours the therapy must meet. This is related to what the modality requires and can vary wildly from 40 hours overall, to weekly therapy for the duration of training, to therapy several times a week throughout training.

Experiencing personal psychotherapy

As a student I have found personal psychotherapy an invaluable resource. I was keen from the first, having read about therapy and gained some superficial insight into how I might find it useful. At times I felt very frightened by returning to education and by what happened in the training group, and my experiences seemed irrational. My therapist helped to soothe me, encouraged me to think through what was happening and to make sense of how the past sometimes impacts on the present. She taught me to soothe myself and to continue to think, even when my feelings seemed overwhelming. This has enabled me to regain clarity of thought when client work has reminded me strongly of my own past experiences and I have felt flooded with feeling. My therapist has consistently offered me support, and worked with me to identify, experience and release my feelings. I learned to trust her, and gradually to trust myself. She affirmed any changes I made and celebrated my successes with me.

In therapy I have had a place to work through personal assumptions, prejudices or projections that have been exposed during training. The journey has at times been very demanding. My therapist has challenged my passivity and the underlying motives for decisions I have taken, personally and professionally. A quote from my journal:

I had therapy today. I am now like an inside out rubber glove – where there were dips there are ridges, my self may be recognisable but feels completely different. I have never experienced such a serious challenge to my way of viewing my self, my clients, and the world.

Sometimes I have hated her and blamed her for what I was feeling, but looking back I have always come to a place where I can understand the value of her intervention and why I wanted to pull away. Experiencing the difficult times, when it would have been easy to leave therapy. The relief and joy of resolution has helped me to

> *(Continued)*
>
> understand how hard it can be for my clients to stay with the process, especially when I am challenging them to change.
>
> Therapy facilitated my finding a depth and a breadth of understanding of my self the student, the client, the therapist and the person. I believe that this has had a profound effect on the way I manage my practice, and on the therapeutic relationships I develop with my clients.

Training structure

Time frame

The majority of trainings are offered on a part-time basis, sometimes with the exception of NHS courses. This gives trainees the opportunity to continue with their normal daily work and develop either a new branch of an existing career path or a totally new career. Depending on the modality being studied, the four components – theoretical study, clinical practice, supervision and personal psychotherapy – take place at separate times. Sometimes theory and supervision are initially offered at the same time when the amount of client work is small.

In planning study time, students need to take account of the amount of time they will need for:

- Taught modules
- Private study, including both reading and the preparation of written work
- Client work – this generally increases with each year of study
- Supervision
- Personal psychotherapy
- Final assessment

As the course progresses demands increase. When applying for a course it is always a good idea to ask for guidance about the overall time frame as well as that for each year of study. Often, the time needed to complete any final assessments, such as a dissertation, may add a further year to the overall length of the course.

Practice settings

1 PRACTICE AS PART OF A NORMAL DAILY WORK SCHEDULE Where the student is planning to integrate psychotherapeutic knowledge and skills into their existing career, client work of a different genre will generally be

a part of the usual daily schedule. It is important to keep clear boundaries between client relationships that form part of normal agency work and those that are psychotherapeutic ones. Both kinds of relationship cannot be maintained by the same person because psychotherapeutic boundaries are very different from almost any other kind. A strong boundary prevents confusion, misunderstanding and difficulties which can easily occur if roles and responsibilities become entangled. It is always advisable to ensure that for those clients seen for psychotherapy all other roles for which the agency or service is responsible are held by other colleagues.

2 ESTABLISHING A NON-WORKPLACE-BASED TRAINING PRACTICE Generally, training placements outside the workplace take place on a voluntary basis on the premise that there is a fair mutual exchange between the service providing clients and rooms in which to see them and the novice psychotherapist setting out to gain experience and expertise. As the placement progresses and the student gains skill and competence some services will either make a contribution towards supervision fees or offer sessional fees. Others will definitely not. And there are some notable examples of services being offered to the public by a continuous population of unrecompensed trainees.

A number of settings offer excellent opportunities to gain therapeutic experience. Top of the list are GP practices. Here there is:

- a wide range of referral problems
- a properly managed, professional setting with procedures for supporting the student and their client in the case of unforeseen difficulties
- the opportunity to work alongside those in allied disciplines
- increasingly, an established therapeutic service for the student to become part of – this helps develop a stronger sense of professional identity than when the student is working in isolation from others in their discipline

Apart from GP surgeries, there is a wide range of voluntary agencies working in the fields of mental health and emotional well-being that can offer the trainee psychotherapist an excellent starting point. Examples include Mind, Cruse and Samaritans.

3 INDEPENDENT PRIVATE PRACTICE Lastly, a comment on practising privately at the start of training. Independent private practice often involves a lone psychotherapist working from either a room in their own home or from hired consulting rooms. The kind of professional

conditions that are part and parcel of either a dedicated psychotherapeutic service or a psychotherapy service based in a GP practice are absent. In this situation the pitfalls for the new student are numerous. Examples of these include:

- intrusive noises from family or other third parties
- inadequate public liability insurance
- unprofessional surroundings such as clients using a family bathroom instead of a dedicated facility
- trying to move between domestic and professional tasks in breaks between clients
- failing to notice where domestic circumstances impinge

> I recall a client telling me with horror about her first visit to a new psychotherapist. From the consulting room window she was able to clearly see intimate items of clothing drying on the washing line in the garden. She never went back.

Assessment

Most courses operate a policy of continuous assessment for theoretical and clinical work, together with an end-of-course dissertation or extended piece of written work. Some also require a final assessment of clinical work, just prior to accreditation. This is to ensure that the candidate's abilities are commensurate with those expected of a qualified psychotherapist. The personal psychotherapy of the candidate is not normally assessed, although it is quite normal to ask for verification from the candidate's therapist that the required amount of appropriate therapy has taken place.

Costs

Training is expensive. If a student is funding themselves they need to look realistically at how they will manage the commitment. Most courses do all they can to help. For example the taught course component is often paid for on a year-by-year basis and it is often possible to pay in instalments through standing order rather than paying in a single lump sum.

Similarly, with supervision and personal psychotherapy a 'pay as you go' system often operates. Many students fund their training through career development loans which, again, can be very helpful. From the point of financial planning it is important to realise that in the immediate pre-qualification period most students are either receiving financial recompense for their work or help from their placement with costs of supervision. Investing in psychotherapy training is a financial investment in one's future career and the long-term view has to be taken on the eventual benefits that will normally come from this.

Curricula

Course curricula vary according to the modality being studied. In general terms studies will incorporate:

- Models or descriptions of the person
- Descriptions of human behaviour and interaction
- Human development from birth to maturity
- Psychopathology
- Ethics and professional practice
- Psychotherapy research
- Cultural and social difference

Students learn methodologies that are linked to the specific approach they are studying.

When selecting a course it is important to choose one whose approach is in keeping with one's own personal style and philosophy so that there is congruence between learning, personal approach and intervention with clients.

A personal experience of training as a psychotherapist

Psychotherapy training is diverse and challenging. There are standard academic elements, but the more significant part is learning through experience: personal therapy, being in a training group and supervised work with clients. My experience of myself and of the world around me changed significantly through seven years. I learned new ideas and skills and enhanced awareness of myself and others. Learning came through having myself and my work scrutinised from every angle. For long periods of time I felt exposed and found this terrifying and exhilarating in equal measure. I believe that this is fundamental to psychotherapy training: exposure is a central experience of every psychotherapy client. Learning this first hand provided the tool that I use most as a psychotherapist – the ability to be myself and to know how I am in relation to others.

I trained for seven years. This is a long time to train, and to succeed I needed the support of trainers, therapy, other students and my

---

(Continued)

partner. At times I felt burned out, and each year I wondered what on earth I was doing. There were milestones along the way that helped keep me going – such as obtaining a postgraduate diploma at the end of year four that allowed me to start charging for my practice. However, demands on time and energy often pushed other personal and professional commitments into second place. This created friction with my partner in particular and together we had to learn how to manage this. As a result we became closer, but it was never easy, and the financial cost of training placed a further strain on us. The need to work whilst training allowed little time for other pursuits. Professional fees are not yet commensurate with psychotherapy training and the ongoing professional development required. This has deterred me from working full time as a psychotherapist.

I experienced losses as a result of training. I lost friends with whom I no longer fitted. I lost my old self that was comfortable and functioned well in the world. I gave up my old secure professional identity in order to become part of a profession still in its formative stages.

But the gains have outweighed the losses. I enjoy my work, and I find the whole process of working with clients deeply satisfying. I have found a profession that offers the opportunity for lifelong stimulation and development. I have made better friends and professional relationships than I had before, and I am more confident and at ease with life. Psychotherapy training embraces life in all its complexity, and once I committed to it, there was no going back.

Career

Starting to build a career

1 PRACTISING WITHIN A PRE-EXISTING WORK SETTING Starting to build a career as a psychotherapist usually begins in the later stages of training. If the student is planning to practise within an existing work setting they will probably already have a well-established client group by the time they are ready for professional accreditation. The context of their practice and their collegial networks are also likely to be well delineated. Generally, building on a pre-existing professional role and reputation makes the consolidation of one's standing as a recognised psychotherapist a relatively easy and straightforward matter. Basic collegial trust already exists and the 'getting to know you and your work' stage has already taken place. Depending on the setting and first training there are still, however, hurdles to jump.

In the NHS nurses, occupational therapists, psychiatrists and psychologists are the most likely to undertake psychotherapy training.

Unsurprisingly, the nearer the top of the hierarchy, the more freedom and choice the psychotherapist tends to have in determining the nature of their practice and the easier it is to gain recompense commensurate with training. Nurses and occupational therapists tend to struggle more to be paid on a scale that they perceive as 'fair'. They are paid much less to deliver psychotherapeutic services than, say, a doctor who has become a consultant psychotherapist. This is not surprising. The hybrid nature of psychotherapy training and its lack of state regulation make this unusual situation possible.

Outside the NHS things are often easier. Voluntary and private agencies as well as some public sector bodies such as social services, often have more fluid employment structures which makes it easier for psychotherapists to gain promotion and salary increases based on their recent qualifications.

Working in the NHS as a core profession psychotherapist without a medical qualification

I am an integrative psychotherapist currently working within a Child and Family Psychiatric Outpatient Department with young people and their families.

Competent and caring psychiatrists who are very supportive of psychotherapy theory and practice manage the department and I am line managed by a psychoanalytic psychotherapist. I feel very valued, supported and respected in my work as a psychotherapist with young people and their parents by my managers and colleagues and I have considerable freedom in developing new ways of working, which is both exciting and rewarding.

However, although I am being employed to provide psychotherapy my job title is that of 'Therapist' and I am paid on the nursing pay scale. My hospital employers want me to provide psychotherapy treatment but will not call me a psychotherapist as this means they would have to pay me on a higher scale. I feel devalued by this. I have trained for many years so that I could work as and be employed as a psychotherapist. No other professional who has undergone intensive training would accept not being described by their proper title and paid appropriately. If I were placed on an equivalent pay scale I would be satisfied and have the possibility in the future of moving up that scale. This is important to me as I am still relatively young in my career.

I like working in the NHS as not only do I have flexible working conditions which help me with childcare but also I am proud to provide psychotherapy that is free at the point of delivery to people who could

---

(Continued)

not normally afford it. The lack of consistent formal recognition of our profession could mean experienced psychotherapists will move away from the NHS. I was at one point tempted by a job with a private fostering agency who would have acknowledged my profession in both job title and pay scale. At the moment I enjoy my current job and am learning so much from it that I have chosen to stay. Ideally, I would want to stay in this department for many years because I know I am fortunate to work in such a supportive environment, for the families I would like to provide a consistency of service. Sadly, however, I cannot see myself staying unless things change.

---

2 ESTABLISHING A NEW PRACTICE SETTING   Initially this is the harder thing to do. But again, by the point of qualification those students in this situation will have been working towards this goal for some time and will generally have a solid base on which to build further. The most common approach is to work sessionally in a variety of settings, for example, primary care, voluntary agencies and privately. Some sessional work is based on employee status and other on self-employed status.

At this point the graduate often has to take on the responsibilities of self-employment. Those with no prior experience in this area can find this rather daunting. There are some simple basic pointers to remember.

- Advice before action – seek professional advice about what will need to be done **before** doing anything
- Accountant – find a respected accountant whose fees are reasonable
- Grants – look round for grants that may be available to help in the setting up of a practice

To work effectively in private practice the psychotherapist needs to create a consulting area that is a professional dedicated space. This can be achieved in a variety of ways. Some of the most popular are:

- Renting rooms in a centre with professionals in similar or allied fields, such as a complementary health centre
- Working with other psychotherapists in a dedicated setting
- Setting aside a part of one's home as a practice area or adding an extension to provide suitable facilities

It is important to have effective sources of referral if a private practice is to be sustainable in the long term. Some people opt for one or two strong sources such as a local psychiatrist or GP. Others prefer to create a wide range of referral sources. In deciding how to approach this matter, psychotherapists need to decide what kind of practice they wish to maintain. If, for example, a psychiatrist is a major referral source clients are more likely to have clearly diagnosable mental health problems of some severity. By contrast, if referrals come from a range of settings client presenting problems are likely to be broader. The place of practice can also have a major bearing on the nature of problems people present. To work in a fashionable part of a metropolis is to invite a very different clientele from that where premises are based in either an inner city or rural area.

Setting up a private practice – financial considerations

This is an apocryphal tale that is told in one of the clinics where I practise. Once every nine years every practitioner will have one day when every appointment is cancelled. As psychotherapists we charge for cancellations made without due notice. However, this tale introduces perhaps the most problematic aspect of setting up a practice, namely money and financial security. The practice has to pay.

Whilst working in Primary Care I had a never-ending list of referrals without any effort on my part. This is not the case in private practice. A colleague telephoned me just after she had started her private practice. Her first words were 'clients leave, that's great, but I need new ones!' This perhaps is stating the obvious, but it is a worrying experience in the first months of private practice. The very essence of what we do as professionals can seem to conflict with our need to be financially secure. The psychotherapist is always working to make themselves redundant by supporting a client to resolve their conflicts so that they can continue their lives without coming for therapy. So the therapy ends and we psychotherapists have to find new clients so that we can continue at the same level of income. The only thing to do is to ensure that you have sufficient additional sources of income to support you throughout the early days of private practice and really work on gaining referrals. I have seen colleagues struggling financially, becoming despondent and giving up their practice where they have failed to do this.

The struggle for me in the early days was simply to ask for my fee. I was used to a situation where I either worked voluntarily or was paid by the NHS. I had never directly asked for money from a client. In my private practice, I would often just forget to mention money. Over and over again in the first week of the therapy the client would leave

(Continued)

without paying. This can, of course, be sorted out the next week. But this in itself is stressful and causes anxiety for the psychotherapist. I lost more clients in the first few weeks of starting a private practice than I have done in the remaining eight years!

An example of learning by experience happened when a colleague told me that she did not negotiate discounted fees. She said that in her experience she often found the person really had sufficient income and that this became apparent as the therapy progressed. This seemed harsh to me, but it did give me cause for thought. Shortly after this conversation I negotiated a discount of £5 per session with a new client. Listening to her circumstances, I was comfortable that this arrangement was fair and would make the difference between her being able to afford psychotherapy and not. It later transpired that she was taking taxis to and from the sessions, despite very good public transport systems. Travelling home on the tube, it struck me that I could not afford a taxi home! This incident taught me a lot about things I needed to check next time round before deciding whether I would be willing to negotiate a lower fee with a client.

It is hard work but enormously rewarding to be running your own practice and be responsible for your own case load. It can also be tremendously isolating. I was therefore determined to work from a clinic rather than from home. Looking for a room to work from was a bewildering and sometimes alarming experience. I came across clinics with pricing structures so complex I felt confused. One clinic I considered required that the practitioners remained in their room even if they did not have a client!

I inadvertently caused a problem at one clinic when they asked for my qualifications and insurance details – a usual practice. I enquired out of interest about their existing psychotherapist's training and philosophical approach. This led to further enquiry within the clinic. It emerged that the so-called psychotherapist had no qualifications and had been on a weekend workshop for coaching skills. His contract was terminated immediately and the clinic tightened up their procedures.

The only guide to finding the right kind of clinic is to talk with the other practitioners, to look at the interaction between the clinic and their clients, and not to lock yourself into a long contract until you are really sure you will be happy there. I have stayed in the same two clinics for five years now and have remained content. One is based in a prestigious location and is dedicated to making money, the other is based in a more modest area and managed by a man who just wants nice people around him. They are both professional settings with high standards of practice and I am happy in both.

Working as a psychotherapist

Working as a psychotherapist is a rich and rewarding experience. It is humbling to be trusted to help a fellow human being with their innermost hopes, fears and aspirations. At its best, the feeling of helping someone to find a way forward when they had previously thought this impossible is deeply moving. At worst, the psychotherapist feels the pain, frustration and grief of those times when the client is so locked into their difficulties that they see no way out and feel deep despair. The rewards of the work extend far beyond the monetary into the emotional and, sometimes, spiritual.

Ethical and professional practice

In working with vulnerable adults and/or children the psychotherapist has to work to the highest ethical and professional standards. Accountability has to be high and any aspect of the therapist's practice should be open to honest appraisal and scrutiny by other colleagues and the public at large. All registered psychotherapists work to strict codes of ethics and practice which describe best practice and provide means of complaint where clients or colleagues are not satisfied with how things have been done and want other members of the profession to look into potential problem areas. Where there has been a clear and gross violation of a professional boundary addressing this is comparatively straightforward to recognise and address. But, as with many things in life, situations are often not clear cut. 'Grey' areas are inevitable and it is these that cause most heartache both for clients and their therapists.

Life-long learning

What can psychotherapists do to ensure their own good practice and continuing rigorous self-evaluation? Everyone knows how easy it is, once student days are behind, to allow bad habits to creep in. Ongoing supervision of case work is one of the best ways to monitor and further the development of good practice. Most psychotherapy organisations and modalities insist on this as part of life-long learning for the duration of practice. One or two do not and take the view that qualification means an end to the need for external scrutiny. I think this is a mistaken view and belongs to a time early in the history of the profession when those practising were medical doctors and enjoyed a sense of public veneration that saw people as patients who were grateful to be treated. By and large society has moved beyond this notion of mindless acquiescence and so should the profession.

Alongside supervision, continuing professional development (CPD) requires practitioners to keep up to date with new thinking and developments in the field. Conferences, private study and advanced seminars are just some of the ways in which professional psychotherapists can do this. Although this may sound onerous it can in fact be very pleasurable to 'go back to the classroom' and network with others in your field who are doing the same thing. New professional friendships are often forged during a coffee break or at the lunch table of a conference.

Peer review of learning

One of the ways the profession ensures practitioners are keeping effectively up to date is to monitor their continuing professional development through its member organisations. A common model is to require an annual statement of learning undertaken and at the fifth year to require the completion of a full audit and review of these activities by a group of peers. Out of this review may come suggestions, requirements or recommendations about how the psychotherapist should approach their future learning.

Peer review is an important form of self-regulation by the profession with four key aims to:

- ensure practitioners keep up to date with new theories and ideas
- ensure therapists are using sound methods of practice
- monitor personal circumstances and ensure they are conducive to continuing practice and therapists are not, for example, hampered by ill health
- create public confidence that the practice of registered psychotherapists is properly monitored and scrutinised

Peer support

Peer support is vital in offsetting one of the most difficult parts of practising as a psychotherapist, the sense of isolation that can occur. It is well documented that isolation is a major cause of stress and anxiety in psychotherapists. The reasons for this are varied. The work itself can be isolating because of the strict confidentiality boundaries which mean psychotherapists can only discuss the detail of their work with a very limited number of people – usually supervisor, case or line manager. The format of the work also creates problems of isolation. Spending long periods of time alone with one other person where all your own wants and needs are put aside in the service of empathically attending to those of others is demanding. The normal 'chit-chat' of say an office environment where work is interspersed with social contact is missing from the psychotherapeutic setting. On top of this, the quality of attention paid to the client must be first-rate most of the time. This is a tall order for anyone. Next, factor-in the likelihood that the psychotherapist works largely alone or in circumstances where there are few other therapists around and the reasons for feelings of isolation becoming compellingly obvious.

Peer support can and should be achieved in a variety of ways so that it forms a cocooning web to support and sustain the psychotherapist in most normal situations that may occur. Some of these ways are:

- Forming peer discussion groups to review new theories, methods and ideas
- Identifying a close and trusted colleague who will be a peer-supervisory support offering advice quickly if the regular supervisor is unavailable
- Finding a peer with whom reciprocal arrangements can be set up to provide locum cover during holiday periods or times of illness
- Selecting a peer with whom to be a reciprocal executor should illness or other circumstances mean clients need to be helped to find an interim therapist because their own will be unavailable for an extended period of time, or, in the case of death, in perpetuity

Diversification

Once a practice has been established and is running smoothly it is important to think about the next development – diversification. It is simply not sustainable over years and years to work in one way only. The psychotherapist becomes jaded when they do this and, whether or not they recognise it, responds less effectively to their clients. It is vital to identify a range of ways in which to work. For example, if a practice is predominantly with individual clients branching out into some group work, perhaps with a co-leader, can make a refreshing change. Sometimes experienced psychotherapists become supervisors and tutors on training courses. Others apply their knowledge to a variety of settings: for example, management training, or working within the legal system, providing reports or expert witness. The opportunities to develop a diverse, interesting and rewarding practice are increasing rapidly as the public expectation that any service it requires (psychotherapeutic or otherwise) should be delivered efficiently and to a high standard. The general move to privatisation across a huge range of services from prisons to medicine has had a big impact. A new climate exists which supports initiative, enterprise and creativity.

What is it like to be working as a psychotherapist?

Working as a psychotherapist is both challenging and rewarding. The choice of being self-employed and managing my own private practice and/or being part of a team liaising with other staff have varied and different responsibilities. Working in a range of settings has broadened my horizons and contributed to my professional development. I find it interesting and stimulating to work with adults. Although it can be frustrating at times when clients are resistant to change, clients' personalities, their presenting problems and the fulfilment of seeing them achieve their aims is very satisfying. Creating my own working environment in private practice, in the way I like and believe is best, allows me to care not only for the client, but for myself as well. I can choose my working hours and days and charge fees that take this into account.

In general, working alone at home, or renting a room by oneself is much harder and can be isolating. I have felt cut off at times as I do not have the recognition, status, salary and benefits that are supported by an organisation, nor can I benefit from close-knit influential team support when faced with a difficult situation. I am constantly concerned about regular client work to sustain my financial needs. The cost of self-promotion, marketing and the cost of supervision are ongoing economic considerations, notwithstanding the practical issues of providing a dedicated therapy room for clients. The possibility of violence or other unacceptable behaviour is an occupational hazard for any psychotherapist, so I ensure that I always have somebody nearby in the unlikely event that I might need help.

Looking after my health is a top priority. Taking sick leave means disruption to clients, as well as loss of income. After many years in the same home I have just moved. This has meant re-establishing my private practice and concurrently trying to find others in an employed capacity whilst I built up my case load again. This was not easy.

My psychotherapy qualifications and the prestige of belonging to a professional body leaves me feeling privileged. The recognition of psychotherapists as health professionals is continually developing and something I want to be part of.

I enjoy working as a psychotherapist. As well as regular supervision, I can have support through my professional body and can also discuss issues with a network of peers if needed. My work provides me with opportunities for both personal and professional development and enables me to value the importance of my own fulfilment.

Working as a psychotherapist is a highly rewarding experience. The depth of training needed to be able to do this effectively is powerful and life-changing in its own right, and is essential to support excellent post-qualification practice.

7

FUTURE TRENDS AND DEVELOPMENTS

CHRISTINE LISTER-FORD

In looking towards the future of the profession there are a number of themes that stand out as important:

- The protection of the client through clearer generic standards and clear channels of accountability
- Re-thinking provision of psychotherapy, in both the NHS and the private sector
- Developing practice and method so that psychotherapy can have greater applicability across social and cultural groups
- Looking at ways to embed therapeutic principles in daily life

Protecting the public

As we saw in Chapter 6, the position of psychotherapy as a profession is anomalous. On the one hand the title 'psychotherapist' is not protected and so anybody can call themselves a psychotherapist. On the other, training as a psychotherapist is seen as a route to consultant status within the NHS for both psychiatrists and psychologists.

In order to protect the public, the profession must be able to set out uniformly high standards of approach and practice using these as a stepping stone for developing into a distinct core profession. The United Kingdom Council for Psychotherapy (UKCP) is the only organisation that regards psychotherapy as a core profession and also takes an umbrella approach to provision, regulation and monitoring. As a profession, psychotherapy must achieve internal homogeneity by creating generic, core standards that provide a coherent and recognisable set of professional parameters. These need to be understandable to the public and provide benchmarks for competency and good practice. They should include:

- A standardised approach to initial training that is common to all schools
- Common standards for post-qualification practice and assessment

- Criteria for further advanced training and life-long learning
- A central complaints and disciplinary body that is separate from all colleges and schools and contains a significant lay membership

Historically, regulation of psychotherapists was recommended as far back as 1978 by Paul Sieghart when he published the outcome of a working party on the subject. His paper recognised these gaps in good practice nearly 30 years ago! Three years later, in April 1981, Graham Bright MP brought a bill to regulate psychotherapy. Unfortunately this bill failed. More recently, at the initiative of UKCP, talks with Lord John Alderdice and other professional organisations resulted in Lord Alderdice bringing a psychotherapy bill to the House of Lords in May 2000. Regrettably this bill also failed.

Finally, in 2004 the Department of Health made funding available for a mapping project for the psychotherapy and counselling professions to chart their standards and consider a regulatory framework. Reasons for this governmental sea change were rooted in a number of factors, perhaps one of the most powerful being the 'Shipman Inquiry' (2005) into the serial killing of patients by general practitioner Harold Shipman. The need for tighter monitoring and regulation of all healthcare services was a compelling outcome of the inquiry. This conclusion drew attention to the need for a range of professional groups to re-think their systems of audit and accountability. Psychotherapy was one of these professions. The importance of psychotherapists being demonstrably accountable for the quality of their work was seen as having national relevance and, for the first time, funds were made available to the profession to help audit and mapping and the move to standardisation.

Establishing core curricula

Because training has evolved piecemeal as psychotherapeutic schools have been established, agreeing core curricula looks complicated at face value. However, I do not think the problem is as big as it may first appear. In fact a plausible pathway was inadvertently opened up several years ago. In an interesting exercise during the 1990s the UKCP set up a working group to draft generic core competencies for psychotherapists across all of the psychotherapeutic modalities that were represented by the then eight sections of the Council. The intention was to provide a framework for a National Vocational Qualification (NVQ). The approaches encompassed were as diverse as hypno-psychotherapy on the one hand and psychodynamic psychotherapy on the other. What emerged surprised everyone. Psychotherapists from across the range of approaches were able to agree on the core competencies needed in a well-trained and proficient psychotherapist. The key area of agreement was the primacy of the quality of the therapeutic alliance. The relationship between client and psychotherapist was the defining factor, viewed as essential by all schools in helping positive therapeutic outcome. Research findings strongly support this view.

These standards, which have lain mothballed for so long, could be an important starting point for looking at the creation of generic training criteria and a common syllabus that begins with similarity and sees difference as more relevant for advanced specialism, post-qualification.

A recognisable name

Currently, all psychotherapists preface their title 'Psychotherapist' with a modality-based descriptor – *integrative, gestalt, cognitive, psychoanalytic* and so forth. These descriptors are very important to the professional but leave the public perplexed and asking questions like *'What do they mean?'*

Why do psychotherapists insist on having all these different names? The answer to this question is bound up with identity and perhaps goes back to Freud himself, who was rigorous in maintaining the integrity of his own theories and approach. As part of this legacy, many later theorists who chose to develop their own approach (for example, Perls with Gestalt, Rogers with Person Centred, and Berne with Transactional Analysis) had to battle hard to establish their schools as reputable. Perhaps because it was so difficult for those who came after Freud to stake their claim to their own way they, and their descendants, have clung tenaciously to their hard-earned differences, and hence the plethora of names.

A second part of the reason for the abundance of names is connected with current psychotherapy training schools which emphasise their differences and the distinctive nature of their approach. Graduates are usually encouraged to take pride in the distinguishing nature of their training and to look at how it may place them in a professionally advantageous position. Since the NHS favours only a small number of modalities and generally limits employment to psychotherapists using these approaches (particularly cognitive behavioural, psychodynamic/analytic approaches and family therapy), the perception that asserting difference is a good idea is encouraged (probably without any real intent) by a major employer.

The dilemma is complex. If psychotherapists give up their defining names some of them may lose important employment opportunities or a feeling of identity that comes from being part of a particular school. But, if they do not find real ways to achieve a common character that includes an identifiable name, psychotherapists risk being seen as a fragmented collection of groups whose main aim is self-protection and self-advancement. An undeclared union rather than a core profession.

To go forward the profession will either need to have a limited number of adjectival descriptors which clarify and explain differences that genuinely have meaning, or it will need to use a single label – 'Psychotherapist'. Other professions solve this dilemma with the use of a single label that is described according to the sphere of practice – 'educational psychologist', 'forensic psychiatrist' and so forth. Psychotherapy will need to find its own set of simple, clear and unambiguous names.

Provision of psychotherapy

Location
Although psychotherapy is more widely available now than at any other time, national provision is still patchy and tends to be dependent on:

- geographical location
- the policy of the local NHS trust
- the ability to pay for choice

Geographically, psychotherapists are most densely clustered in London and the south and then in the cities and large towns of the UK. UKCP registrants, for example, are to be found as follows:

London	2,001
North East	458
North West	792
Scotland	221
South East	1,829
South West	583
Wales	189

However, despite these obvious clusterings, it is usually possible to find a psychotherapist within a reasonable travelling distance even in some more remote locations.

NHS provision
Within the NHS, psychotherapy provision is generally time limited ranging from brief intervention of between one and six sessions to

long-term intervention which is usually about a year. Anything beyond a year is still unusual. Provision is reliant on local trust policy and the specialist interests of the consultants who are in post. In the NHS, psychotherapy is generally seen as a specialist treatment for enduring mental health problems such as a personality disorder. It is more often found as part of secondary rather than primary service provision. A limited number of approaches are generally offered, notably cognitive behavioural, psychodynamic and family and systemic.

At primary care level, talking therapies in the NHS are generally recognised as being delivered by counsellors, psychologists and nurse specialists. Services are invariably described as 'counselling' rather than 'short-term psychotherapy'. There is often a functional confusion in primary services about what is counselling and what is psychotherapy. Some of the confusion arises because clear descriptions comparing and contrasting the two disciplines are not easy to find. This is due to the failure of the professions to clearly articulate the distinct but overlapping nature of the two fields. And, as we have already seen, confusion is also created by the way NHS posts and pay scales are structured. Many qualified psychotherapists work in primary care delivering time-limited therapy, but as we saw in the last chapter they are not called psychotherapists, rather they are often called counsellors and seen to be providing counselling. Dedicated psychotherapy services are not the norm at primary level.

The provision of a coherent, rational psychotherapy service within the NHS is clearly desirable and something the profession should be, and is, pursuing. However, realistically, it is unlikely to be achieved (even with statutory regulation) in the foreseeable future. The complexity of the problems inhibiting it are too great both from the point of NHS hierarchical structures which delineate role and task in a linear not horizontal way, and, of course, because (as we have seen) the profession is still far from providing a coherent description and account of itself. These problems will need long-term solutions.

The private sector

In the private sector, a wide range of types of psychotherapy is readily available. A would-be client can not only select from a rich diversity of schools but has much greater choice about the length and frequency of their therapy as well as the mode – individual, group, couples, family, child, and so forth. Increasing numbers of therapists are approved by medical insurance companies so that clients with healthcare plans are often able to access psychotherapy through their provider. And, of course, the ability to 'shop around' for the right psychotherapist is normally easy to do. A client who is in a position to fund their own psychotherapy enjoys wider and richer options than a client who lacks the resources to do this.

In the private sector difficulties sometimes occur if practitioners drop their standards of basic good practice. For example, although it is usual for many psychotherapists to base their private practice from home, some do not make proper separation between the domestic and the professional. Basic professional facilities should include a separate waiting area equipped with all the usual facilities and a separate entrance. The client should not be aware of any aspect of the therapist's domestic circumstances impinging on them; for example, family noises (children playing), family sights (washing drying), family smells (supper cooking). The integrity of the therapeutic space depends on the proper containment of these kinds of things. Clients can easily feel they are a nuisance or less important than something in the therapist's home life. In these situations a variety of undesirable and non-therapeutic issues may arise. For example, a client may feel resentful that their time and privacy is impinged upon but feel unable to say anything for fear their therapist won't like it. Another possibility is that a client seeing a domestic problem feels the need to try and look after their therapist by trying to help solve the problem.

A further difficulty that can occur with private practice is the qualification of the therapist. As we have seen, the name 'psychotherapist' is an unprotected label that anyone can use. This means that those looking for a personal psychotherapist need to check that the person they choose is properly qualified and registered. This is most easily done by referring to the relevant register.[1]

A second issue to be aware of is that many training schools allow their students to set up in private practice prior to qualification. In such circumstances the candidate in training should make their trainee status clear and their fee should reflect their lack of qualification and experience. Would-be clients should ask to see written verification from the training school that their trainee is working appropriately under close supervision.

My own view about both these issues is that the profession will need to review its position and reassess the basis of sound professional practice. Certainly in the first half of the twentieth century those training in psychotherapy were quite often established professionals in medicine. Setting up in private practice on this basis was, perhaps, more acceptable. In today's climate practical experience is more helpfully gained in properly established professional settings where not only is there help on hand should it be needed, but also proper monitoring of students' work. It should no longer be an option for the unqualified trainee to set up in private practice. The profession will need to take up this issue as part of the work on establishing standards of good practice for the future. I hope it will see the value of setting guidelines about the overall management of private practice that include appropriate settings as well as qualification of practitioners. Increasingly, psychotherapists working privately are seeing the need to establish their base in a professional setting such as a bespoke centre. This is a trend to be supported and encouraged by the profession.

Client groups

Traditionally, psychotherapy has been seen as a 'talking cure' for the white middle class. To stay dynamic and responsive to social need it needs to look at how therapeutic intervention can be creatively tailored to a multiplicity of social needs and a wide range of therapeutic services made available. Psychotherapists need to be proactive in reaching out to different social groups, initiating dialogue with them about what they would find useful and then developing psychotherapeutic services accordingly. I would like to look at two groups that might be considered: one is white, non-middle class; the second is black ethnic minority groups. I am not happy about describing this second group in this way because I realise that it represents an unacceptable clumping together of a diverse range of cultural and social groups. However, since the project I am to describe has, as a first step, found it best to identify itself in this way, I follow suit.

Child and single parent

In recent years there has been an increase in the number of single parents. Where single parenthood is characterised by economic or social difficulty, need can often become so pressing that children and their parents require the help of social and legal services to provide protection, support and care. Typically, these services do not have provision for, or access to, psychotherapeutic resources. In the work that my colleagues and I have done with single-parent families we have found that therapeutic assessment and timely intervention can have a profound impact. In many cases it can make the difference between children and their parents either being able to continue to live together with support, or retain positive contact on a regular basis, rather than family difficulties reaching such a pitch that only separation of the child from their parent can ensure safety for the child. We have found family lawyers and courts increasingly interested in therapeutic assessment and intervention.

Case example

Karen, a 29-year-old mother of six, had, herself, a disrupted and painful childhood. Through poor parenting in her own childhood that was more due to incompetence than a desire to hurt, she had experienced neglect, lack of protection and mistreatment. At a tender age she soon became the 'little mother' to her own alcoholic mother. As many do, she went on to seek the love and comfort she craved from her own parents in her relationships with her own children. Unwittingly repeating the patterns of mothering she, herself, had experienced in childhood she failed to mother her own children adequately. One by one her children were taken from her and placed in the care of the local authority. When Zack, her sixth child, was born, everything was set for the usual painful legal procedures that would end in the protective removal of her son and freeing for adoption. However, a new social worker took an innovative approach and decided to see what could be done to help Karen become the good enough mother she said she wanted to be. Karen began working with a psychotherapist to develop awareness of some of the patterns and behaviours from her own childhood that were affecting her approach to mothering. Zack was placed in foster care but with the intention that Karen would have ready supervised access to him so that she could build her mothering skills and, hopefully, show herself to be a good enough mother. Karen worked hard to change. And although there were ups and downs, overall she made some real improvements. After a year it was decided that Zack could begin to spend some time each week at home with Karen with the view that, if things went well, this time could increase.

As Zack grew into a feisty toddler a second therapist worked with Karen and Zack together to help Karen learn the all-important skills of playing with her son effectively and thereby building the bonds of a healthy and positive relationship. Careful monitoring of Karen by her social worker provided supervision of the progress of her relationship with her son. By the time Zack was three years old it was decided that the work had been successful and that Karen had developed sufficiently adequate new attitudes and skills as a mother to enable Zack to be removed from the 'at risk' register, and for mother and child to live together supported by social services and psychotherapeutic intervention.

Comment

This work was only made possible by the readiness of the various agencies to take a ground-breaking approach to Zack's protection and long-term best interests and to look again at Karen's motivation and ability to change. Leading-edge use of funding sources was also required. In fact, the cost of the psychotherapeutic help given to Karen and Zack turned out to be several thousands of pounds less than the cost of legal proceedings would have been to remove him from Karen's care and place him in an adoptive family. In this particular situation everyone benefited – Zack, Karen and society at large.

Karen and Zack's story is an example of what can be achieved with psychotherapeutic help when the human circumstances of the child and his mother are promising, the statutory bodies are willing and able to be innovative in their approach and there is a good relationship between the psychotherapist and the agencies that includes a realistic view of the parameters of what can be undertaken and achieved.

Of course, not all children and their parents can or should stay together. Sometimes circumstances are such that the best option is for separation. But even in these heart-breaking circumstances psychotherapy can be of help in working through the anger, pain and loss of separation. It can help parents come to terms with their grief in a supported and contained way. Although circumstances cannot be changed people are less alone with their pain when they have a caring therapist to bear witness to their anguish and to the depth of their distress. In supportive circumstances, those grieving are less likely to turn to old habits that were perhaps part of their difficulty in the first place such as alcohol, drugs, violence or reckless spending.

Depending on the age of the child and the circumstance of their placement it is invariably advisable to consider psychotherapeutic help for the child either by supporting a carer or adopting parent to take a planned therapeutic approach to the loss of attachment to the parent or by providing direct therapeutic input for the child. Even a child as young as three or four can derive enormous benefit from psychotherapy that is geared to their age range. I have seen a young child use a sand tray and a toy figure he chose that clearly represented his mother, spend over 15 minutes burying and resurrecting the figure in the sand. His grief and despair were palpable. After this session his carer reported that he was calmer than he had been in a long time.

Ethnic diversity

Psychotherapy has often failed to respond effectively to diverse ethnic and cultural need. White and Westernised are the traditional cultural assumptions underpinning most psychotherapeutic practice.

Psychotherapeutic theories have not attempted to understand or respond to cultural difference in any coherent or comprehensive way. The profession could be justly criticised for taking a 'one size fits all' approach sustained by an implicit attitude that if it doesn't fit that's too bad. Whilst there are obviously many individual exceptions to this, there has been minimal research into how theories might respond to cultural diversity and how methodologies could be developed to respond more effectively to the wide range of social mores. The profession still fails to attract significant numbers of students from the range of ethnic groups to train as psychotherapists. Without this direct link with communities and cultures there is little hope of change. Professional associations and individual schools need to develop effective strategies for attracting students from a wide range of cultural groups.

The Sakhi[2] project is an example of an innovative approach to brief intervention at primary care level. Eighteen months old, the project is a unique transcultural service, the culmination of ten years' community engagement by the black voluntary sector and service users in the North East of England. It demonstrates a case for locating integrative psychotherapy for black and ethnic minority communities (including refugees and asylum seekers) at the heart of a primary and social care agenda to tackle inequalities in health. Sakhi offers dedicated bilingual brief psychotherapy to people who normally would not access this as an alternative to medication or psychiatry. Alongside this it will provide transcultural mental health training to clinicians working with diverse communities. Recognising that few people in the North East from black and minority ethnic communities access psychotherapy within primary care, Sakhi offers humanistically integrative and transcultural models of therapeutic support, working with existing providers to develop a multilinguistic and culturally competent service.

Cultural competence in the therapeutic context is marked by the following indicators:

- Is there community involvement in planning, development and assessment?
- Does decision making by the service incorporate the experiences and aspirations of the community?
- Are clients educated as to their expectations and rights?
- Is the environment in which the service is delivered welcoming and attractive and based on the diversity of its clients?
- Is the service based on measurable outcomes rather than on stereotypes?

- Do all staff understand that 'one size does not fit all'?
- Do staff reflect the diversity of the communities they serve?
- Do staff revisit models of delivery in the light of demographic changes and service testing?
- Are staff consistent and creative in communicating with black and minority ethnic patients and their communities?
- Does the service uphold its legislative responsibilities and liabilities?

The service is already well used and its client base continues to grow. There is an overwhelming need for the development of many similar services for diverse ethnic groups nationwide.

Applying psychotherapeutic principles to daily living

The notion of applying psychotherapeutic principles to daily living is not new. From Moreno and his experiments with psychodrama[3] to the gestaltists to Claude Steiner's experiments with 'emotional literacy' in the 1960s and 1970s, the idea that an awareness of the principles and practice of making good relationships, as well as an understanding of how groups work, could be useful in a variety of social, educational and organisational settings has often been to the forefront. However, as with so much about the extended application of psychotherapeutic principles, many of the early experiments occurred in a spirit of creativity and isolation from one another. Many of them shone their light and then faded, often to be re-invented at another time. Examples of this kind of re-invention are the so-called new ideas of 'emotional literacy' campaigns and 'sharing circles' now commonly used in many of our schools to help children appreciate and be responsive to each other's experiences and feelings. These ideas are not new. They were at the forefront of the thinking of transactional analysts over 30 years ago. Emotional literacy is based on the idea that we each assume emotional responsibility for ourselves by owning our actions, recognising our hidden motivations and feelings, and are proactive about meeting our own needs. These were some of the so-called radical ideas of the human potential movement of the 1960s and 1970s. By the 1980s these ideas had lost some of their impetus and slowly faded from awareness as the move to new forms of power, notably power dressing, and power living – being able to 'have it all' and do it all captured the popular imagination.

In this new millennium there is a realisation that we cannot have it all, be it all and do it all. This is a naïve, self-centred view that depletes resources, commodifies relationships and makes for unhappiness.

People suffer. We have seen social problems intensify – increasing numbers of our young people become addicted to drugs; swathes of the population cannot afford to purchase their own homes and there is no prospect on the horizon of being able to do so; the National Health Service increasingly cannot find the resources to provide for its patients as waiting times become greater and the wherewithal to provide care diminishes. The re-emergence of the recognition of the need for 'emotional literacy' is seen as part of the solution to these problems. As a society we need people to take ownership of themselves and their actions; we have to help ourselves as well as receive assistance. What can psychotherapy offer? At their most useful, psychotherapeutic ideas can help provide preventative strategies and approaches to re-establish some of the emotional connectivity that much of our society has lost. I would like to look further at the sphere of education to consider what can be done to build emotional literacy.

Training all teachers in therapeutic principles and skills to help them build emotional awareness and resilience in children would be a major step forward but not a significant departure from existing teacher training curricula. Many aspects of developmental psychology as well as training in communication are already taught. To extend the scope of what is taught to include further input would be relatively straightforward. Areas that might be included are:

- Models of the person that describe human experience – the easily understood but highly sophisticated Parent–Adult–Child model[4] would be ideal
- Models of communication that combine the social and the psychological such as Transactions from transactional analysis[5]
- Techniques for helping individual children as well as groups of children understand their feelings and their associated behaviour and its impact on others

Making such knowledge a part of core teacher training curricula and a part of core curricula in schools would help ensure that developing and maintaining emotional awareness and interpersonal sensitivity become embedded in our educational approach and were not simply an add-on whose efficacy was of more unpredictable value.

An example of how this might work in practice comes from one of my colleagues who was a teacher to a class of seven-year-olds in an inner city school. The use of aggression and intimidation as the means for resolving difficulties was common practice amongst the children. The children often intimidated, bullied and hurt each other and, in the process, themselves, too of course. My colleague agreed with the children to begin each day with a sharing circle when the children could talk about things that were bothering them and get help both from their teacher and the other people in the class to resolve them. It was also an opportunity for them to 'boast' about things they had done well or were pleased about. In addition she gave brief inputs over each week about some of the topics I have listed above. By the end of the first term the children's behavioural problems had improved radically. They showed themselves competent in confronting each other and were often tougher than an adult might have been. At the end of the academic year the children moved to a new class teacher who did not use these techniques. My colleague saw a rapid return to 'old ways' within three months.

Whilst it is upsetting to know that the children were not able to continue with their new ways, it underlines the vital role the teacher played in providing a safe place for them to openly talk and share and find new ways to solve difficulties and highlights gains to be found by joining psychotherapeutic principles and educational practice.

Conclusion

Psychotherapy is a profession in change. It offers a rich and diverse resource which is highly adaptable and can be used to advance many aspects of life and living. As a profession it is undergoing arguably the most radical metamorphosis since the mid-twentieth century. Having come a long way it still has far to go and much to develop.

Notes

1. Most registers can be easily accessed online, examples include: United Kingdom Council for Psychotherapy – ukcp.org.uk; British Confederation of Psychotherapists – bcp.org.uk.

2. My thanks to Shehla Naqvi, who leads the service, for providing me with this information.

3. Marineau, R.F., *Jacob Levy Moreno 1889–1974: Father of Psychodrama, Sociometry and Group Psychotherapy* (London, Routledge, 1989).

4. Lister-Ford, C., *Skills in Transactional Analysis Counselling and Psychotherapy* (London, Sage, 2002).

5. Ibid.

REFERENCES

Chapter 1

Alexander, F. and French, T. (1946) *Psychoanalytic Therapy: Principles and Application.* New York: Ronald Press.

Arkowitz, H. (1991) 'Introductory statement: psychotherapy integration comes of age', *Journal of Psychotherapy Integration*, 1(1): 1–3.

Arkowitz, H. (1992) 'Integrative theories of therapy', in D.K. Freedheim (ed.), *History of Psychotherapy: A Century of Change.* Washington, DC: American Psychological Association.

Arkowitz, H. (1997) 'Integrative theories of therapy (revised)', in P.L. Wachtel and S.B. Messer (eds), *Theories of Psychotherapy: Origins and Evolution.* Washington, DC: American Psychological Association.

Arnkoff, D.B. and Glass, C.R. (1995) 'Cognitive therapy and psychotherapy integration', in D.K. Freedheim (ed.), *History of Psychotherapy: A Century of Change.* Washington, DC: American Psychological Association.

Barr, J. (1987) 'Therapeutic relationship: the interpersonal model', *Transactional Analysis Journal* 17(4).

Beck, A.T. (1976/1991) *Cognitive Therapy and the Emotional Disorders.* London: Penguin.

Beisser, A. (1970) 'The paradoxical theory of change', in J. Fagan and I.L. Shepherd (eds), *Gestalt Therapy Now.* New York: Harper Colophon.

Berne, E. (1961/2001) *Transactional Analysis in Psychotherapy.* London: Souvenir Press.

Bowlby, J. (1969/1989) *Attachment and Loss.* London: Penguin.

Bowlby, J. (1988) *A Secure Base.* London: Routledge.

Bowlby, J. (1994) *The Making & Breaking of Affectional Bonds.* London: Routledge.

Buber, M. (1923/2004) *I and Thou.* London: Continuum International Publishing Group.

Cain, D.J. and Seeman, J. (eds) (2001) *Humanistic Psychotherapies: Handbook of Research and Practice.* Washington, DC: APA Publications.

Clarkson, P. (1992) *Transactional Analysis: An Integrated Approach.* London: Routledge.

Clarkson, P. (1995) *The Therapeutic Relationship.* London: Whurr.

Davies, D. and Charles, N. (eds) (1996) *Pink Therapy: Guide for Counsellors Working with Lesbian, Gay and Bisexual Clients.* Maidenhead: Open University Press.

Dollard, J. and Miller, N.E. (1950) *Personality and Psychotherapy: An Analysis in Terms of Learning, Thinking and Culture.* New York: McGraw-Hill.

Dryden, W. (2000) 'Rational emotive behavioural therapy', in C. Feltham and I. Horton (eds), *Handbook of Counselling and Psychotherapy.* London: Sage.

Eagle, M.N. and Wolitsky, D.L. (1992) 'Psychoanalytic theories of psychotherapy', in D.K. Freedheim (ed.), *History of Psychotherapy: A Century of Change.* Washington, DC: American Psychological Association.

Ellenberger, H.F. (1970) *Discovery of the Unconscious: The History and Evolution of Dynamic Psychiatry.* New York: Basic Books.

Ellis, A. (1962/1995) *Reason and Emotion in Psychotherapy*. New York: Citadel.

Ernst, S. and Goodison, L. (1981) *In Our Own Hands: A Book of Self-help Therapy*. London: The Women's Press.

Erskine, R.G. (1993) 'Inquiry, attunement, and involvement in the psychotherapy of dissociation', *Transactional Analysis Journal*, 23: 184–90.

Eysenck, H.J. (1952) 'The effects of psychotherapy: an evaluation', *Journal of Consulting Psychology*, 16: 319–24.

Eysenck, H.J. (1959) 'Learning theory and behaviour therapy', *Journal of Mental Science*, 105: 61–75.

Fairbairn, W.R.D. (1952) *Psychoanalytic Studies of the Personality*. London: Tavistock Publications and Routledge & Kegan Paul.

Feltham, C. and Horton, I. (2000) *Handbook of Counselling and Psychotherapy*. London: Sage.

Ferenczi, S. and Rank, O. (1925/1986) 'The development of psychoanalysis: monograph 4 of the Chicago Institute of Psychoanalysis Classics', in G. Pollock (ed.), *Psychoanalysis Monograph Series*. Madison, CT: International Universities Press.

Fishman, D.B. and Franks, C.M. (1992) 'Evolution and differentiation within behaviour therapy: a theoretical and epistemological review', in D.K. Freedheim (ed.), *History of Psychotherapy: A Century of Change*. Washington, DC: American Psychological Association.

Frankl, V. (1946/2004) *Man's Search for Meaning*. London: Rider.

Freud, S. (1913) *On Beginning the Treatment*. The Standard Edition of the Complete Psychological Works of Sigmund Freud, Vol. 12. London: Hogarth Press.

Freud, S. and Breuer, J. (1895/1974) *Studies on Hysteria*. The Pelican Freud Library, Vol. 3. Harmondsworth: Penguin.

Glass, C.R. and Arnkoff, D.B. (1995) 'Behavior therapy', in D.K. Freedheim (ed.), *History of Psychotherapy: A Century of Change*. Washington, DC: American Psychological Association.

Goulding, M.M. and Goulding, R.L. (1979) *Changing Lives Through Redecision Therapy*. New York: Brunner Mazel.

Greenberg, L., Rice, L. and Elliott, R.K. (1993) *Facilitating Emotional Change: The Moment-by-moment Process*. New York: Guilford Press.

Guidano, V.F. and Liotti, G. (1983) *Cognitive Processes and Emotional Disorders: A Structural Approach to Psychotherapy*. New York: Guilford Press.

Guntrip, H. (1969/1992) *Schizoid Phenomena, Object Relations and the Self (Maresfield Library)*. London: Karnac.

Hargaden, H. and Sills, C. (2002) *Transactional Analysis Psychotherapy*. London: Brunner/Routledge.

Hoffman, D. (2003) 'Sándor Ferenczi and the origins of humanistic psychology', *Journal of Humanistic Psychology*, 43: 59–86.

Holmes, J. and Bateman, A. (2002) *Integration in Psychotherapy*. Oxford: Oxford University Press.

Hycner, R. (1985) 'Dialogical Gestalt therapy: an initial proposal', *Gestalt Journal*, 8: 23–49.

Hycner, R. and Jacobs, L. (1995) *The Healing Relationship in Gestalt Psychotherapy*. New York: Gestalt Journal Press.

Ingerman, S. (1991) *Soul Retrieval: Mending the Fragmented Self*. San Francisco: Harper SF.

Jacobs, L. (1989) 'Dialogue in Gestalt theory and therapy', *Gestalt Journal*, 12: 25–68.

Janet, P. (1889) *L'Automatisme psycholoqique*. Paris: Flix Alcan.

Jaspers, K. (1913/1959) *General Psychopathology* (7th edn, trans. J. Hoenig and M.W. Hamilton). Manchester: Manchester University Press.

Jung, C.G. (1936/1959) 'The concept of the collective unconscious', in *The Collected Works of C.G. Jung*, Vol. 9, Part 1. London: Routledge. pp. 42–53.

Kirchenbaum, H. (1979) *On Becoming Carl Rogers*. New York: Delacorte.

Klein, M. (1935/1984) 'A contribution to the psychogenesis of manic-depressive states', in H. Segal (ed.), *Introduction to the Work of Melanie Klein*. London: Hogarth. (Reprinted Karnac, 1988.)

Kohut, H. (1971) *The Analysis of the Self*. New York: International Universities Press.

Kohut, H. (1984) *How Does Analysis Cure?* Chicago: University of Chicago Press.

Lapworth, P., Sills, C. and Fish, S. (2001) *Integration in Counselling and Psychotherapy: Developing a Personal Approach*. London: Sage.

Lazarus, A. (1958) 'New methods in psychotherapy: a case study', *South African Medical Journal*, 32: 660–4.

Lazarus, A. (1967) *The Practice of Multimodal Therapy*. New York: McGraw-Hill.

Linehan, M.M. (1993) *Cognitive Behavioural Treatment of Borderline Personality Disorder*. New York and London: Guilford Press.

Linke, S. (1999) *Psychological Perspectives on Traditional Jewish Practices*. New York: Aronson.

Lomas, H. (1985/2005) 'The development of the BABCP', in *BABCP Handbook*. Accrington: BABCP.

Lovell, K. (2000) 'Behavioural psychotherapy', in C. Feltham and I. Horton (eds), *Handbook of Counselling and Psychotherapy*. London: Sage.

Mahoney, M.J. (1990) *Human Change Processes: Theoretical Bases for Psychotherapy*. New York: Basic Books.

Maccoby, M. (1995) 'Review of L. Aron and A. Harris (1993) *The Legacy of Sándor Ferenczi*. Hillsdale, NJ: The Analytic Press', in *Psychoanalytic Psychology*, 12: 321–3.

McLellan, B. (1995) *Beyond Psychopression*. Melbourne: Spinifex Press.

Messer, S.B. (1992) 'A critical examination of belief structures in integrative and eclectic psychotherapy', in J.C. Norcross and M.R. Goldfried (eds), *Handbook of Psychotherapy Integration*. New York: Basic Books. pp. 130–68.

Miller, A. (1981/1985) *Thou Shalt Not Be Aware*. London: Pluto Press.

Milton, J., Polmear, C. and Fabricius, J. (2004) *A Short Introduction to Psychoanalysis*. London: Sage.

Murray, D.J. (1995) *Gestalt Psychology and the Cognitive Revolution*. London: Harvester Wheatsheaf.

Neimeyer, R.A. (1986) 'Personal construct therapy', in W. Dryden and L. Golden (eds), *Cognitive-behavioural Approaches to Psychotherapy*. London: Harper & Row. pp. 224–60.

Palmer, S. and Woolfe, R. (eds) (1999) *Integrative and Eclectic Counselling and Psychotherapy*. London: Sage.

Parlett, M. (1991) 'Reflections on field theory', *British Gestalt Journal*, 1: 69–81.

Pavlov, I. (1903) 'The experimental psychology and psychopathology of animals', at the 14th International Medical Congress, Madrid. Cited in *Nobel Lectures, Physiology and Medicine 1901–1921* (1967). Amsterdam: Elsevier.

Perls, F., Hefferline, R.F. and Goodman, P. (1951/1990) *Gestalt Therapy: Excitement and Growth in the Human Personality*. London: Souvenir Press.

Robertson, J. and Robertson, J. (1969) *John, Aged Seventeen Months, for Nine Days in a Residential Nursery*. 16 mm, 43 minutes. Young Children in Brief Separation Film Series. Concord Video and Film Council, Ipswich.

Rogers, C. (1951/1990) *Client Centred Therapy*. London: Constable.

Rogers, C. (1961/1989) *On Becoming a Person*. London: Constable.

Rogers, C. (1978) *On Personal Power*. London: Constable.

Rosenzweig, S. (1936) 'Some implicit common factors in diverse methods in psychotherapy', *American Journal of Orthopsychiatry*, 6: 412–15.

Rowan, J. (1983) *The Reality Game*. London: Routledge.

Rowan, J. (1993) *The Transpersonal: Psychotherapy and Counselling*. London: Routledge.

Rowan, J. and Jacobs, M. (2002) *The Therapist's Use of Self*. Maidenhead: Open University Press.

Ryle, A. (1982) *Psychotherapy: A Cognitive Integration of Theory and Practice*. London: Academic Press.

Schore, A.N. (2003) *Affect Regulation and the Repair of the Self*. New York: Norton.

Siegel, A. (1996) *Heinz Kohut and the Psychology of the Self*. London: Sage.

Skinner, B.F. (1938/1999) *The Behavior of Organisms: An Experimental Analysis*. Cambridge, MA: B.F. Skinner Foundation.

Skinner, B.F. (1948/1976) *Walden Two*. New York: Macmillan.

Stein, H.T. (ed.) (2003) 'Basic principles of classical Adlerian psychology', in *The Collected Clinical Works of Alfred Adler: Volume 3*. Bellingham, WA: Classical Adlerian Translation Project.

Stein, H.T. and Edwards, M.E. (1998) 'Classical Adlerian theory and practice', in P. Marcus and A. Rosenburg (eds), *Psychoanalytic Versions of the Human Condition: Philosophies of Life and their Impact on Practice*. New York: New York University Press.

Stricker, G. (1994) 'Reflections on psychotherapy integration', *Clinical Psychology: Science and Practice*, 1: 3–12.

Sullivan, H.S. (1953) *The Interpersonal Theory of Psychiatry*. New York: Norton.

Tallis, F. (1998) *Changing Minds: The History of Psychotherapy as an Answer to Human Suffering*. London: Cassell.

Van Deurzen-Smith, E. (1997) *Every Day Mysteries*. London: Routledge.

Wachtel, P.L. (1977) *Psychoanalysis and Behaviour Therapy: Towards an Integration*. New York: Basic Books.

Watson, J.B. (1913) 'Psychology as the behaviorist views it', *Psychological Review*, 20: 158–77.

Wellings, N. and McCormick, E.W. (eds) (2000) *Transpersonal Psychotherapy: Theory and Practice*. London: Sage.

Winnicott, W.D. (1958/1992) *Through Paediatrics to Psychoanalysis*. London: Karnac.

Wolfe, B.E. (1995) 'Self pathology and psychotherapy integration', *Journal of Psychotherapy Integration*, 5: 293–312.

Yontef, G.M. (1993) *Awareness, Dialogue and Process: Essays on Gestalt Therapy*. Highland, NY: Gestalt Journal Press.

Chapter 2

Bulmer, L. (2003) 'An integrative psychotherapy treatment pathway for a patient diagnosed with lower level borderline personality disorder who deliberately self-harms'. Unpublished MSc Dissertation, University of Wales.

Clarkson, P. (1992) 'A multiplicity of therapeutic relationships as a principle of integration', in P. Clarkson, *Transactional Analysis Psychotherapy*. London: Routledge.

Collins (1999) *Collins English Dictionary: A Millennium Edition*. London: Harper Collins.

Cooper, C. (2002) 'Psychodynamic therapy: the Kleinian approach', in W. Dryden (ed.), *Handbook of Individual Therapy*. London: Sage.

Dryden, W. (2001) *Reason to Change: A Rational Emotive Behaviour Therapy Workbook*. London: Brunner/Routledge.

Johnson, S. (2000) 'Kate: a study of the escalation of self-harm in a borderline patient admitted to hospital'. Unpublished MSc Dissertation, University of Wales.

Malan, D. (1979) *Individual Psychotherapy and the Science of Psychodynamics*. Oxford: Butterworth Heinemann.

National Institute for Clinical Excellence – NICE (2005) www.nice.org.uk

Norcross, J.C. and Grencavage, L.M. (1990) 'Eclecticism and integration in counselling and psychotherapy, major themes and obstacles', in W. Dryden and J.C. Norcross (eds), *Eclecticism and Integration in Counselling and Psychotherapy*. Loughton: Gale Centre Publications.

Nuttall, J. (2002) 'Imperatives and perspectives on psychotherapy integration', *International Journal of Psychotherapy*, 7(3): 249–64.

Rowan, J. (2001) *Ordinary Ecstasy: The Dialectics of Humanistic Psychology* (3rd edn). London: Brunner/Routledge.

Safran, J. and Messer, S. (1997) 'Psychotherapy integration: a postmodern critique', *Clinical Psychology: Science and Practice*, 4: 140–52.

Shah, I. (2004) 'Relational functioning in clients diagnosed with borderline personality disorder'. Unpublished MSc Dissertation, University of Wales.

Stark, M. (2000) *Modes of Therapeutic Action*. New York: Aronson.

Wills, F. and Sanders, D. (1997) *Cognitive Therapy: Transforming the Image*. London: Sage.

Chapter 3

American Psychiatric Association (1980) *Diagnostic and Statistical Manual of Mental Disorders*, 3rd edn. Washington, DC: American Psychiatric Association.

American Psychiatric Association (1994) *Diagnostic and Statistical Manual of Mental Disorders*, 4th edn. Washington, DC: American Psychiatric Association.

American Psychological Association Task Force on Psychological Intervention Guidelines (1999) *Template for Developing Guidelines. Interventions for Mental Disorders and Psychosocial Aspects of Physical Disorders*. Washington, DC: American Psychological Association.

Arkowitz, H. (1992) 'Integrative theories of therapy', in D.K. Freedheim (ed.), *History of Psychotherapy: A Century of Change*. Washington, DC: American Psychological Association. pp. 261–303.

Asay, T.P. and Lambert, M.J. (1999) 'The empirical case for the common factors in therapy: quantitative findings', in M.A. Hubble, B.L. Duncan and S.D. Miller (eds), *The Heart and Soul of Change: What Works in Therapy*. Washington, DC: American Psychological Association. pp. 33–55.

Bachelor, A. and Horvath, A. (1999) 'The therapeutic relationship', in M.A. Hubble, B.L. Duncan and S.D. Miller (eds), *The Heart and Soul of Change: What Works in Therapy*. Washington, DC: American Psychological Association. pp. 133–78.

Barkham, M. (2002) 'Methods, outcomes and processes in the psychological therapies across four successive research generations', in W. Dryden (ed.), *Handbook of Individual Therapy*, 4th edn. London: Sage. pp. 373–433.

Barkham, M., Stiles, W.B., Hardy, G.E. and Field, S.D. (1996) 'The assimilation model; theory, research and practical guidelines', in W. Dryden (ed.), *Research in Counselling and Psychotherapy: Practical Applications*. London: Sage. pp. 1–24.

Barlow, D.H., Hayes, S.C. and Nelson, R.O. (1984) *The Scientist-practitioner: Research and Accountability in Clinical and Educational Settings*. Oxford: Pergamon Press.

Baxter, L.J., Schwartz, J.M., Bergman, K.S., Szuba, M.P., Guze, B.H., Mazziotta, J.C., Alazraki, P.A., Selin, C.E., Ferng, H.K., Munford, P. and Phelps, M. (1992) 'Caudate glucose metabolic rate changes with both drug and behavior therapy for obsessive-compulsive disorder', *Archives of General Psychiatry*, 49(9): 681–9.

Beecher, H.K. (1955) 'The powerful placebo', *Journal of the American Medical Association*, 159(17): 1602–6.

Berger, R. and Mallison, R. (2000) 'Therapeutizing research: the positive impact of family-focused research on participants', *Smith College Studies in Social Work*, 27: 307–14.

Bergin, A.E. (1971) 'The evaluation of therapeutic outcomes', in A.E. Bergin and S.L. Garfield (eds), *Handbook of Psychotherapy and Behavior Change: An Empirical Analysis*. New York: Wiley. pp. 217–70.

Bergin, A.E. and Garfield, S.L. (1994) 'Overview, trends and future issues', in A.E. Bergin and S.L. Garfield (eds), *Handbook of Psychotherapy and Behavior Change*, 4th edn. New York: Wiley. pp. 821–30.

Bergin, A.E. and Lambert, M.J. (1978) 'The evaluation of therapeutic outcome', in S.L. Garfield and A.E. Bergin (eds), *Handbook of Psychotherapy and Behavior Change*, 2nd edn. New York: Wiley. pp. 139–90.

Beutler, L. E. and Crago, M. (eds) (1991) *Psychotherapy Research: An International Review of Programmatic Studies*. Washington, DC: American Psychological Association.

Beutler, L.E., Machado, P.P.M. and Allstetter Neufeldt, S.A. (1994) 'Therapist variables', in A.E. Bergin and S.L. Garfield (eds), *Handbook of Psychotherapy and Behavior Change*, 4th edn. New York: Wiley. pp. 229–69.

Bischoff, R., McKee, A., Moon, S. and Sprenkle, D. (1996) 'Therapist-conducted consultation: using clients as consultant to their own therapy', *Journal of Marital and Family Therapy*, 22(3): 359–79.

Bohart, A.C., O'Hara, M. and Leitner, L.A. (1998) 'Empirically violated treatments: disenfranchisement of humanistic and other psychotherapies', *Psychotherapy Research*, 8(2): 141–57.

Bordin, E.S. (1979) 'The generalisability of the psychoanalytic concept of the working alliance', *Psychotherapy: Theory, Research and Practice*, 16: 252–60.

Bower, P. and King, M. (2000) 'Randomised controlled trials and the evaluation of psychological therapy', in N. Rowland and S. Goss (eds), *Evidence-based Counselling and Psychological Therapies: Research and Applications*. London: Routledge. pp. 79–110.

Brody, A.L., Saxena, S., Stoessel, P., Gillies, L.A., Fairbanks, L.A., Alborzia, S. et al. (2001) 'Regional brain metabolic changes in patients with major depression treated with either paroxetine or interpersonal therapy: preliminary findings', *Archives of General Psychiatry*, 58(7): 631–40.

Butler, S.F. and Strupp, H.H. (1986) 'Specific and non-specific factors in psychotherapy: a problematic paradigm for psychotherapy research', *Psychotherapy*, 23: 30–40.

Cain, D.J. and Seeman, J. (eds) (2001) *Humanistic Psychotherapies: Handbook of Research and Practice*. Washington, DC: American Psychological Association.

Chambless, D.L. (1996) 'In defence of dissemination of empirically supported psychological interventions', *Clinical Psychology: Science and Practice*, 3: 230–5.

Courchesne, E., Chisum, H. and Townsend, J. (1994) 'Neural activity-dependent brain changes on development: implications for psychopathology: the role of early experience and plasticity', *Development and Psychopathology*, 6(4): 697–722.

Critelli, J.W. and Neumann, K.F. (1984) 'The placebo: conceptual analysis of a construct in transition', *American Psychologist*, 39(1): 32–9.

Damasio, A. (1994) *Descartes' Error*. New York: Grossett/Putnam.

Department of Health (1996) *NHS Psychotherapy Services in England: Review of Strategic Policy*. London: HMSO.

Elkin, I. (1994) 'The NIMH Treatment of Depression collaborative research study', in A.E. Bergin and S.L. Garfield (eds), *Handbook of Psychotherapy and Behavior Change*, 4th edn. New York: Wiley. pp. 114–39.

Elkin, I., Shea, M.T., Watkins, J.T., Imber, S.D., Sotsky, S.M., Collins, J.F., Glass, D.R., Pilkonis, D.A., Leber, W.R., Docherty, J.P., Fiester, S.J. and Parloff, M.B. (1989) 'National Institute of Mental Health treatment of depression collaborative research program: general effectiveness of treatment: where we began and where we are', *Archives of General Psychiatry*, 46(11): 971–82.

Elliot, R. (2001) 'The effectiveness of humanistic therapies: a meta-analysis', in D.J. Cain and D. Seeman (eds), *Humanistic Psychotherapies: Handbook of Research and Practice*. Washington, DC: American Psychological Association. pp. 57–81.

Elliot, R. and Shapiro, D.A. (1992) 'Client and therapist as analysts of significant events', in S.G. Toukmanian and D.L. Rennie (eds), *Psychotherapy Process Research: Paradigmatic and Narrative Approaches*. London: Sage.

Etherington, K. (2000) *Narrative Approaches to Working with Adult Male Survivors of Sexual Abuse: The Clients', the Counsellor's and the Researcher's Story*. London: Jessica Kingsley.

Etherington, K. (ed.) (2001) *Counsellors in Health Settings*. London: Jessica Kingsley.

Etherington, K. (ed) (2002) *Rehabiliation Counselling in Physical and Mental Health*, London: Jessica Kingsley.

Eysenck, H.J. (1952) 'The effects of psychotherapy: an evaluation', *Journal of Consulting Psychology*, 16(5): 319–24.

First, M.D, Bell. C.C. Culhbert, B., Krystal, J.H., Malison, R., Offord, D.R. et al. (2002) Personality disorders and relational disorders: a research agenda for addressing crucial gaps in DSM', in D.J. Kupfer, M.B. First and D.A. Regier (eds), *A Research Agenda for DSM-V*. Washington, DC: American Psychiatric Association. pp. 123–99.

Frank, J.D. (1961) *Persuasion and Healing: A Comparative Study of Psychotherapy*. Baltimore: Johns Hopkins University Press.

Frank, J.D. (1973) *Persuasion and Healing: A Comparative Study of Psychotherapy*, 2nd edn. Baltimore: Johns Hopkins University Press.

Frank, J.D and Frank, J.B. (1991) *Persuasion and Healing: A Comparative Study of Psychotherapy*, 3rd edn. Baltimore: Johns Hopkins University Press.

Frank, J.D., Gliedman, L.H., Imber, S.D., Stone, A.R. and Nash, E.H. Jr. (1959) 'Patients' expectancies and relearning as factors determining improvement in psychotherapy', *American Journal of Psychiatry*, 115: 961–8.

Freud, S. (1912) 'On the beginning of treatment: further recommendations on the technique of psychoanalysis', in J. Strachey (ed. and trans.) (1958), *Standard Edition of the Complete Psychological Works of Sigmund Freud*. Vol. 12. London: Hogarth Press. pp. 122–44.

Freud, S. (1913) 'The dynamics of transference', in J. Strachey (ed. and trans.) (1966), *Standard Edition of the Complete Psychological Works of Sigmund Freud*. Vol. 12. London: Hogarth Press. pp. 97–108.

Garfield, S.L. (1987) 'Towards a scientifically oriented eclecticism', *Scandinavian Journal of Behaviour Therapy*, 16: 95–109.

Garfield, S.L. (1994) 'Research on client variables in psychotherapy', in A.E. Bergin and S.L. Garfield (eds), *Handbook of Psychotherapy and Behavior Change*, 4th edn. New York: Wiley, pp. 190–228.

Garfield, S.L. and Bergin, A.E. (1994) 'Introduction and historical overview', in A.E. Bergin and S.L. Garfield (eds), *Handbook of Psychotherapy and Behavior Change*, 4th edn. New York: Wiley. pp. 3–18.

Gelso, C.J. and Carter, J.A. (1985) 'The relationship in counselling and psychotherapy: components, consequences, and theoretical antecedents', *The Counseling Psychologist*, 13: 155–423.

Glaser, B.G. and Strauss, A. (1967) *The Discovery of Grounded Theory*. Chicago: Aldine.

Goldfried, M.R. and Padawer, W. (1982) 'Current status and future directions in psychotherapy', in M.R. Goldfried (ed.), *Converging Themes in Psychotherapy*. New York: Springer. pp. 3–50.

Gordon, T., Grummon, D.L., Rogers, C.R. and Seeman, J. (1954) 'Developing a program of research in psychotherapy', in C.R. Rogers and R.F. Dymond (eds), *Psychotherapy and Personality Change*. Chicago: University of Chicago Press. pp. 12–34.

Goss, S. and Rowland, N.I. (2000) 'Getting evidence into practice', in S. Goss and N.I. Rowland (eds), *Evidence Based Counselling and Psychological Therapies*. London: Routledge. pp. 191–205.

Grafanaki, S. and McLeod, J. (1999) 'Narrative processes in the construction of helpful and hindering events in experiential psychotherapy', *Psychotherapy Research*, 9(3): 289–303.

Greenberg, L.S. and Pinsoff, W.M. (1986) *The Psychotherapeutic Process: A Research Handbook*. New York: Guilford Press.

Greenhough, W.T., Black, J.E. and Wallace, C.S. (1987) 'Experience and brain development', *Child Development*, 58: 539–99.

Horvath, A.O. and Greenberg, L.S. (1989) 'Development and validation of the Working Alliance Inventory', *Journal of Counseling Psychology*, 36(2): 223–33.

Horvath, A.O. and Symonds, B.D. (1991) 'Relation between working alliance and outcome in psychotherapy: a meta-analysis'. *Journal of Counseling Psychology*, 38(2): 139–49.

Howard, G.S. (1983) 'Towards methodological pluralism', *Journal of Counseling Psychology*, 30(1): 19–21.

Howard, K.I., Kopta, S.M., Krause, M.S. and Orlinsky, D.E. (1986) 'The dose–effect relationship in psychotherapy', *American Psychologist*, 41(2): 159–64.

Hubble, M.A., Duncan, B.L. and Miller, S.D. (1999) *The Heart and Soul of Change: What Works in Therapy*. Washington, DC: American Psychological Association.

Jacobson, N.S., Follette, W.C. and Revenstorf, D. (1984) 'Psychotherapy outcome research; methods for reporting variability and evaluating clinical significance', *Behavior Therapy*, 15: 336–52.

Kadera, S.W., Lambert, M.J. and Andrews, A.A. (1996) 'How much therapy is really enough? A session by session analysis of the dose–effect relationship', *Journal of Psychotherapy Practice and Research*, 5: 132–51.

Kazdin, A.E. (1986) 'Research designs and methodology', in S.L. Garfield and A.E. Bergin (eds), *Handbook of Psychotherapy and Behavior Change*. New York: Wiley. pp. 23–68.

Klintsova, A.Y. and Greenough, W.T. (1999) 'Synaptic plasticity in cortical systems', *Current Opinion in Neurobiology*, 9(2): 203–8.

Krupnick, J.L., Stotsky, S.M., Simmons, S., Moyer, J., Elkin, I., Watkins, J. and Pilkonis, P.A. (1996) 'The role of the therapeutic alliance in psychotherapy and pharmacotherapy outcome: findings in the National Institute Mental Health treatment of depression collaborative research program', *Journal of Consulting and Clinical Psychology*, 64: 532–9.

Lambert, M.J. (1992) 'Implications of outcome research for psychotherapy integration', in J.C. Norcross and M.R. Goldstein (eds), *Handbook of Psychotherapy Integration.* New York: Basic Books. pp. 94–129.

Lambert, M.J. and Bergin, A.E. (1992) 'Achievements and limitations of psychotherapy research', in D.K. Freedheim (ed.), *History of Psychotherapy: A Century of Change.* Washington, DC: American Psychological Association. pp. 360–90.

Lambert, M.J., Shapiro, D.A. and Bergin, A.E. (1986) 'The effectiveness of psychotherapy', in S.L. Garfield and A.E. Bergin (eds), *Handbook of Psychotherapy and Behavior Change,* 3rd edn. New York: Wiley. pp. 157–212.

Liggan, D.Y. and Kay, J. (1999) 'Some neurobiological aspects of psychotherapy', *Journal of Psychotherapy Practice and Research,* 8(2): 103–14.

Luborsky, L. (1976) 'Helpful alliances in psychotherapy', in J.L. Cleghorn (ed.), *Succesful Psychotherapy.* New York: Brunner/Mazel. pp. 92–116.

Luborsky, L., Crits-Cristoph, P. and Mellon, J. (1986) 'Advent of objective measures of the transference concept', *Journal of Consulting and Clinical Psychology,* 54(1): 39–47.

Luborsky, L., Diguer, L., Seligman, D.A., Rosenthal, R., Krause, E.E., Johnson, S., Halperin, G., Bishop, M., Berman, J.S. and Schweizer, E. (1999) 'The researcher's own therapy allegiances: A "wild card" in comparisons of treatment efficacy', *Clinical Psychology: Science and Practice,* 6(1): 95–106.

Luborsky, L., Singer, B. and Luborsky, L. (1975) 'Comparative studies of psychotherapies: is it true that "Everybody has won and all must have prizes"?', *Archives of General Psychiatry,* 32(8): 995–1008.

McLeod, J. (1999) *Practitioner Research in Counselling.* London: Sage.

McLeod, J. (2000) 'The contribution of qualitative research to evidence-based counselling and psychotherapy', in N. Rowland and S. Goss (eds), *Evidence-based Counselling and Psychological Therapies: Research and Applications.* London: Routledge. pp. 111–26.

McLeod, J. (2001a) *Qualitative Research in Counselling and Psychotherapy.* London: Sage.

McLeod, J. (2001b) 'Developing a research tradition consistent with the practices and values of counselling and psychotherapy: why counselling and psychotherapy research is necessary', *Counselling and Psychotherapy Research,* 1(1): 3–11.

McLeod, J. (2003) *Doing Counselling Research,* 2nd edn. London: Sage.

McNeilly, C.L. and Howard, K.I. (1991) 'The effects of psychotherapy: a re-evaluation based on dosage', *Psychotherapy Research,* 1(1): 74–8.

Madigan, S. (1999) 'Inscription, description and deciphering chronic identities', in I. Parker (ed.), *Deconstructing Psychotherapy.* London: Sage. pp. 150–63.

Mallincrodt, B. and Nelson, M.L. (1991) 'Counselor training level and the formation of the psychotherapeutic working alliance', *Journal of Counseling Psychology,* 38(2): 133–8.

Marshall, R., Spitzer, R., Vaughan, S., Vaughan, R., Mellman, L., MacKinnon, R. and Roose, S. (2001) 'Assessing the subjective experience of being a participant in psychiatric research', *American Journal of Psychiatry,* 158(2): 319–21.

Martin, S.D., Martin, E., Rai, S.S., Richardson, M.A., Royall, R. and Eng, C. (2001) 'Brain blood flow changes in depressed patients treated with interpersonal psychotherapy or venlafaxine hydrochloride', *Archives of General Psychiatry,* 58(7): 641–8.

Meltzoff, J. and Kornreich, M. (1970) *Research in Psychotherapy.* New York: Atherton Press.

Morrow-Bradley, C. and Elliott, R. (1986) 'Utilization of psychotherapy research by practicing psychotherapists', *American Psychologist,* 41(2): 188–97.

Moustakas, C. (1990) *Heuristic Research: Design, Methodology and Applications.* Thousand Oaks, CA: Sage.

Murray, H.A. (1938) *Exploration in Personality: A Clinical and Experimental Study of Fifty Men of College Age.* New York: New York University Press.

NHS Excecutive (1996) *NHS Psychotherapy Services in England: Review of Strategic Policy.* London: Department of Health.

Norcross, J.C. (1986) 'Eclectic psychotherapy: an introduction and overview', in J.C. Norcross (ed.), *Handbook of Eclectic Psychotherapy.* New York: Brunner/Mazel. pp. 3–24.

Norcross, J.C. and Newman, C.F. (1992) 'Psychotherapy integration: setting the context', in J.C. Norcross and M.R. Goldfried (eds), *Handbook of Psychotherapy Integration,* New York: Basic Books. pp. 3–45.

Orlinsky, D.E. and Russell, R.L. (1994) 'Tradition and change in psychotherapy research: notes on the fourth generation', in R.L. Russell (ed.), *Reassessing Psychotherapy Research.* London: Guilford Press. pp. 185–215.

Orlinsky, D.E., Grawe, K. and Parks, B.K. (1994) 'Process and outcome in psychotherapy – noch einmal', in A.E. Bergin and S.L. Garfield (1994) (eds), *Handbook of Psychotherapy and Behavior Change.* New York: Wiley. pp. 270–376.

Parry, G. (2000) 'Evidence-based psychotherapy: an overview', in N. Rowland and S. Goss (eds), *Evidence-based Counselling and Psychological Therapies: Research and Applications.* London: Routledge. pp. 57–76.

Rennie, D.L. (2001) 'Experiencing psychotherapy', in D.J. Cain and D. Seeman (eds), *Humanistic Psychotherapies: Handbook of Research and Practice.* Washington, DC: American Psychological Association. pp. 117–44.

Rice, L.N. and Greenberg, L.S. (eds) (1984) *Patterns of Change.* New York: Guilford Press.

Rogers, C.R. (1957) 'The necessary and sufficient conditions of therapeutic personality change', *Journal of Consulting Psychology,* 21(2): 95–103.

Rosenwald, G.C. (1988) 'A theory of multiple case research', *Journal of Personality,* 56(1): 239–64.

Rosenzweig, S. (1936) 'Some implicit common factors in diverse methods in psychotherapy', *Journal of Orthopsychiatry,* 6: 412–15.

Roth, A. and Fonagy, P. (1996) *What Works for Whom? A Critical Review of Psychotherapy Research.* London: Guilford Press.

Safran, D., Crocker, P., McMain, S. and Murray, P. (1990) 'Therapeutic alliance rupture as a therapy event for empirical investigation', *Psychotherapy,* 27: 154–65.

Schore, A.N. (2001) 'Minds in the making: attachment, the self-organizing brain, and developmentally oriented psychoanalytic psychotherapy', *British Journal of Psychotherapy,* 17(3): 299–328.

Schwartz, J.M., Stoessel, P.W., Baxter, L.J., Martin, K.M. and Phelps, M.E. (1996) 'Systemic changes in cerebral glucose metabolic rate after successful behavior modification treatment of obsessive-compulsive disorder', *Archives of General Psychiatry,* 53(2): 109–13.

Seligman, M.E.P. (1995) 'The effectiveness of psychotherapy: the Consumer Reports study', *American Psychologist,* 50(12): 965–74.

Shapiro, D.A., Harper, H., Startup, M., Reynolds, S., Bird, D. and Suokas, A. (1994) 'The high water mark of the drug metaphor: a meta-analytic critique of process–outcome research', in R.L. Russell (ed.), *Reassessing Psychotherapy Research.* New York: Guilford Press. pp. 1–35.

Smith, M.L. and Glass, G.V. (1977) 'Meta-analysis of psychotherapy outcome studies', *American Psychologist,* 32(9): 752–60.

Smith, M.L., Glass, G.V. and Miller, T.I. (1980) *The Benefits of Psychotherapy.* Baltimore: Johns Hopkins University Press.

Snyder, C.R. (1994) *The Psychology of Hope: You Can Get There From Here.* New York: Free Press.

Snyder, C.R., McDermott, D., Cook, W. and Rapoff, M. (1997) *Hope for the Journey: Helping Children Through the Good Times and the Bad.* San Francisco: Harper Collins.

Snyder, C.R., Scott, T.M. and Cheavens, J.S. (1999) 'Hope as a psychotherapeutic foundation of common factors, placebos and expectancies', in M.A. Hubble, B.L. Duncan and S.D. Miller (eds), *The Heart and Soul of Change: What Works in Therapy.* Washington, DC: American Psychological Association. pp. 179–200.

Stern, D.N. (1995) *The Interpersonal World of the Infant.* New York: Basic Books.

Stiles, W.B. (2001) 'Future directions in research on humanistic psychotherapy', in D.J. Cain and D. Seeman (eds), *Humanistic Psychotherapies: Handbook of Research and Practice.* Washington, DC: American Psychological Association.pp. 605–16.

Stiles, W.B. and Shapiro, D.A. (1989) 'Abuse of the drug metaphor in psychotherapy process–outcome research', *Clinical Psychology Review,* 9: 521–43.

Stiles, W.B., Elliot, R., Llewelyn, S.P., Firth-Cozens, J.A., Margison, F.R., Shapiro, D.A. and Hardy, G.E. (1990) 'Assimilation of problematic experiences by clients in psychotherapy', *Psychotherapy,* 27(3): 411–20.

Stiles, W.B., Honos-Webb, L. and Surko, M. (1998) 'Responsiveness in psychotherapy', *Clinical Psychology: Science and Practice,* 5: 439–58.

Stiles, W.B., Shapiro, D.A. and Elliot, R. (1986) 'Are all psychotherapies equivalent?', *American Psychologist,* 41(2): 146–80.

Strauss, A. and Corbin, J. (eds) (1997) *Grounded Theory in Practice.* Thousand Oaks, CA: Sage.

Stubbs, J.P. and Bozarth, J.D. (1994) 'The dodo bird revisited: a qualitative study of psychotherapy efficacy research', *Applied and Preventive Psychology,* 3(2): 109–20.

Talley, P.E., Strupp, H.H. and Butler, S.F. (eds) (1994) *Psychotherapy Research and Practice: Bridging the Gap.* New York: Basic Books.

Tallman, K. and Bohart, A.C. (1999) 'The client as common factor: clients as self-healers', in M.A. Hubble, B.L. Duncan and S.D. Miller (eds), *The Heart and Soul of Change: What Works in Therapy.* Washington, DC: American Psychological Association. pp. 91–131.

Watt, D.F. (2003) 'Psychotherapy in an age of neuroscience: bridges to affective neuroscience', in H. Wilkinson and J. Corrigal (eds), *Revolutionary Connections: Psychotherapy and Neuroscience.* London: Karnac. pp. 79–115.

Weinberger, J. (1995) 'Common factors aren't so common: the common factors dilemma', *Clinical Psychology Science and Practice,* 2: 45–69.

Wilkins, W. (1984) 'Psychotherapy: the powerful placebo', *Journal of Consulting and Clinical Psychology,* 52(4): 570–3.

Chapter 4

Albee, G.W. (1990) 'The futility of psychotherapy', *Journal of Mind and Behaviour,* 11(3/4): 369–84.

Alexander, R. (1995) *Folie a Deux: An Experience of One to One Therapy.* London: Free Association Books.

Burchill, J. (2001) 'The whine industry', *The Guardian,* 16 June.

Caine, L. and Royston, R. (2003) *Out of the Dark.* London: Bantam.

Cloud, D. (1998) *Control and Consolation in American Culture and Politics: Rhetoric of Therapy.* Thousand Oaks, CA: Sage.

Elton Wilson, J. (1996) *Time-conscious Psychological Therapy.* London: Routledge.

Epstein, W. (1995) *The Illusion of Psychotherapy.* New Brunswick, NJ: Transaction.

Feltham, C. (1999) 'Facing, understanding and learning from critiques of psychotherapy and counselling', *British Journal of Guidance and Counselling,* 27(3): 301–11.

Fox Gordon, E. (2000) *Mockingbird Years: A Life In and Out of Therapy*. New York: Basic Books.

France, A. (1988) *Consuming Psychotherapy*. London: Free Association Books.

Hetherington, A. (2000) 'A psychodynamic profile of therapists who sexually exploit their clients', *British Journal of Psychotherapy*, 16(3): 274–86.

Hinshelwood, R.D. (1997) *Therapy or Coercion? Does Psychoanalysis Differ from Brainwashing?* London: Karnac.

Holmes, J. (1992) 'Response to Masson, J., *The Tyranny of Psychotherapy*', in W. Dryden and C. Feltham (eds), *Psychotherapy and its Discontents*. Buckingham: Open University Press.

House, R. (2003) *Therapy Beyond Modernity: Deconstructing and Transcending Profession-centred Therapy*. London: Karnac.

James, O. (2003) 'The Cassandra complex', *The Guardian Weekend*, 22 March.

Lomas, P. (1999) *Doing Good? Psychotherapy Out of its Depth*. Oxford: Oxford University Press.

Masson, J. (1984) *The Assault on Truth: Freud and Child Sexual Abuse*. New York: Farrar, Straus & Giroux.

Masson, J. (1997) *Against Therapy*. London: Harper Collins.

McLeod, J. (2000) *Qualitative Research in Counselling and Psychotherapy*. London: Sage.

McNally, R.J. (2003) *Remembering Trauma*. Cambridge, MA: The Belknap Press.

Moustakas, C. (1990) *Heuristic Research: Design Methodology and Application*. London: Sage.

Mowbray, R. (1996) 'Registration: the case against', *Human Potential*, 19 (Autumn).

Panksepp, J. (1998) *Affective Neuroscience. The Foundations of Human and Animal Emotions*. Oxford: Oxford University Press.

Pilgrim, D. (1997) *Psychotherapy and Society*. London: Sage.

Pilgrim, D. and Guinan, P. (1999) 'From mitigation to culpability: rethinking the evidence about therapist sexual abuse', *European Journal of Psychotherapy Counselling and Health*, 2(2): 153–68.

Roth, A. and Fonagy, P. (1996) *What Works For Whom?* London: Guilford Press.

Russel, J. (1993) *Out of Bounds: Sexual Exploitation in Counselling and Therapy*. London: Sage.

Rutter, P. (1990) *Sex in the Forbidden Zone: When Therapists, Doctors, Clergy, Teachers and other Men in Power Betray Women's Trust*. London: Unwin Paperbacks.

Samuels, A. (1993) *The Political Psyche*. London: Routledge.

Sands, A. (2000) *Falling for Therapy: Psychotherapy from a Client's Point of View*. London: Macmillan.

Schore, A. (2003) *Affect Regulation and the Repair of the Self*. New York: Norton.

Smail, D. (1996) *How to Survive without Psychotherapy*. London: Constable.

Spinelli, E. (2001) *The Mirror and the Hammer: Challenges to Therapeutic Orthodoxy*. London: Continuum.

Sunday Times (2003) Leader, 2 March.

Tavris, C. (2003) *Times Literary Supplement*, 15 August.

Chapter 5

American Psychiatric Association (1980) *Diagnostic and Statistical Manual of Mental Disorders 3*. Washington, DC: APA.

American Psychiatric Association (1987) *Diagnostic and Statistical Manual of Mental Disorders 3R*. Washington, DC: APA.

American Psychiatric Association (1994) *Diagnostic and Statistical Manual of Mental Disorders 4*. Washington, DC: APA.

American Psychiatric Association (2000) *Diagnostic and Statistical Manual of Mental Disorders 4TR*. Washington, DC: APA.

Barkham, M. and Mellor-Clark, J. (2000) 'Rigour and relevance: the role of practice-based evidence in psychological therapies', in N. Rowland and S. Goss (eds), *Evidence-based Counselling and Psychological Therapies*. London: Routledge.

Bentall, R.D. (ed.) (1992) *Reconstructing Schizophrenia*. London: Routledge.

Brown, G.W. (1996) 'Life events, loss and depressive disorders', in T. Heller, J. Reynolds, R. Gomm, R. Muston and S. Pattison (eds), *Mental Health Matters*. London: Macmillan/Open University Press.

Browne, D. (1996) 'The black experience of mental health law', in T. Heller, J. Reynolds, R. Gomm, R. Muston and S. Pattison (eds), *Mental Health Matters*. London: Macmillan/Open University Press.

Burton, M. (1998) *Psychotherapy and Counselling in Primary Healthcare*. Chichester: Wiley.

Chalmers, I. (1998) 'Unbiased, relevant and reliable assessments in healthcare', *British Medical Journal*, 3117: 1167–8.

Council for Involuntary Tranquilliser Addiction (CITA) (2002) Telephone information line.

CPForumPC (2001) Counselling and Psychotherapy Forum in Primary Healthcare Training Guidelines document.

Department of Health (1999a) *National Service Framework for Mental Health*. London: HMSO

Department of Health, White Paper (1999b) *Saving Lives: Our Healthier Nation*. London: HMSO.

Department of Health, White Paper (1997) *The New NHS: Modern, Dependable*. London: HMSO.

Department of Health, White Paper (2000) *The NHS: A Plan for Investment, A Plan for Reform*. London: HMSO.

Ellenberger, H. (1970) *The Discovery of the Unconscious: The History and Evolution of Dynamic Psychiatry*. New York: Basic Books.

Gabe, J. (1996) 'The history of tranquilliser use', in T. Heller, J. Reynolds, R. Gomm, R. Muston and S. Pattison (eds), *Mental Health Matters*, London: Macmillan/Open University Press.

Gaffan, E., Tsaousis, I. and Kempwheeler, S. (1995) 'Researcher allegiance and meta-analysis: the case of cognitive therapy for depression', *Journal of Consulting and Clinical Psychology*, 63: 966–80.

Goldberg, D. and Huxley, P. (1992) *Common Mental Disorders*. London: Routledge.

Goldberg, J. (ed.) (1990) *Psychotherapeutic Treatment of Cancer Patients*. New Brunswick, NJ: Transaction.

Gomm, R. (1996) 'Mental health and inequality', in T. Heller, J. Reynolds, R. Gomm, R. Muston and S. Pattison (eds), *Mental Health Matters*. London: Macmillan/Open University Press.

Harrison, G., Owens, D., Holton, A., Neilson, D. and Boot, D. (1988) 'A prospective study of severe mental disorder in Afro-Caribbean patients', *Psychological Medicine*, 18: 643–58.

Herbert, M. (1990) *Planning a Research Project*. London: Cassell.

Kendell, R. (1996) 'The nature of psychiatric disorders', in T. Heller, J. Reynolds, R. Gomm, R. Muston and S. Pattison (eds), *Mental Health Matters*. London: Macmillan/Open University Press.

Kinderman, P. and Cooke, A. (2000) *Recent Advances in Understanding Mental Illness and Psychotic Experiences*. London: British Psychological Society.

Knowles, J. (2005) Chair of the Psychotherapy Faculty of the Royal College of Psychiatrists, personal communication by e-mail.

Kutchins, H. and Kirk, S. (1999) *Making Us Crazy*. London: Constable.

Levitt, R. and Wall, A. (1992) *The Reorganised NHS*. London: Chapman & Hall.

Mind (2004) Report in *The Guardian* newspaper, 13 September.

Parry, G. (2000) 'Evidenced-based psychotherapy: an overview', in N. Rowland and S. Goss (eds), *Evidence-based Counselling and Psychological Therapies*. London: Routledge.

Parry, G. and Richardson, A. (1996) *The Review of Strategic Policy on NHS Psychotherapy Services in England*. London: Department of Health.

Pilgrim, D. and Rogers, A. (1996) 'Two notions of risk in mental health debates', in T. Heller, J. Reynolds, R. Gomm, R. Muston and S. Pattison (eds), *Mental Health Matters*. London: Macmillan/Open University Press.

Robinson, L., Berman, J. and Neimeyer, R. (1990) 'Psychotherapy for the treatment of depression: a comprehensive review of controlled outcome research', *Psychological Bulletin*, 108: 30–49.

Roth, A. and Fonagy, P. (1996) *What Works for Whom? A Critical Review of Psychotherapy Research*. London: Guilford Press.

Sackett, D., Rosenberg, W., Grey, J., Haynes, R. and Richardson, W. (1996) 'Evidenced-based medicine: what it is and what it isn't', *British Medical Journal*, 312: 71–2.

SANE (2004) Report in *The Guardian*, 13 September.

Scott, T. (1994) 'The nature and origins of GPs' attitudes to counselling in general practice', MSc Thesis, University of Surrey.

Scott, T. (1995) *Counselling Integration Research Report*, East Surrey Mental Health and Learning Disabilities NHS Trust.

Scott, T. (1996) 'Health and illness: the new frontier', *Human Potential*, 18: 7–9.

Scott, T. (2004) *Integrative Psychotherapy in Healthcare: A Humanistic Approach*. Basingstoke: Palgrave/Macmillan.

UKCP (1996), Survey of registrants comissioned by Board of Governors.

UKCP/NHS Committee (2002) *Guidelines for Psychotherapy Training for NHS Practice*.

World Health Organisation (1992) *International Classification of Mental and Behavioural Disorders: Clinical Descriptions and Diagnostic Guidelines*. Geneva: WHO.

INDEX